The Melting Pot®

Dip into Something Different®

A collection of recipes from our fondue pot to yours

Dip into Something Different®

The Melting Pot

A collection of recipes
from our fondue pot to yours

Dip into Something Different®

**A collection of recipes from
our fondue pot to yours**

The
Melting Pot®

FRP.

Favorite Recipes® Press

Copyright © 2008 by
The Melting Pot Restaurants, Inc.
8810 Twin Lakes Boulevard
Tampa, Florida 33614
800.783.0867

Executive Editor: Kendra Sartor
Assistant Editor: Misa Julien
Creative Advisor: Jeremy Primm

Cover, food, and equipment photography
by Rutherford Studios
© by The Melting Pot Restaurants, Inc.

Library of Congress Control Number: 2008925490
ISBN: 978-0-9797283-0-3

Favorite Recipes Press is an imprint of FRP, Inc.,
a wholly owned subsidiary of Southwestern/Great American, Inc.
P.O. Box 305142, Nashville, Tennessee 37230
800.358.0560

Art Direction and Book Design: Steve Newman
Project Editor: Tanis Westbrook
Essayist: Molly Kempf

Manufactured in the United States of America
First Printing 2008
15,000 copies

Printed with agri-based inks on recycled paper.

Acknowledgments

The Melting Pot would like to thank its family of passionate, committed, and superior franchise partners…without you this dream would never have become a reality and we would have remained a humble family of four or five fondue restaurants. To our founding fathers of fondue, Bruce Knoechel and Roy Nelson…could you have imagined in your wildest dreams that your little spot in Maitland, Florida, would grow into the nation's premier fondue restaurant concept? To our Franchise Support Center staff…you were the designers and caretakers of this project, our cheerleaders, and our always eager taste testers. To Chef Shane Schaibly and his team of culinary assistants, William Dispenza and Brad Bennett,…for their expertise in recipe compilation and testing. And, most importantly, to our guests…you have kept this fondue dream not just alive, but thriving and growing for more than thirty years. You are the reason we decided to put this collection of fondue recipes together. We hope it brings you hours of enjoyment in your home with your family and friends. We look forward to seeing you soon in our restaurants and hearing all about your fondue adventures at home!

Fonduely Yours,

Mark Johnston

Bob Johnston

Michael Johnston

Dip into Something Different®

From our humble beginnings as a tiny local restaurant with a three-item menu to our current standing as one of America's most elegant niche dining franchises, The Melting Pot has always set the standard for a unique fondue experience with fresh ingredients, a relaxed atmosphere, and attentive service.

At The Melting Pot, fondue becomes an unforgettable four-course meal that you won't find anywhere else. We strive to provide each of our guests with all the ingredients necessary for a Perfect Night Out—no matter what the occasion. Be it a romantic date, a casual get-together with friends and family, or an important business meeting, The Melting Pot is always the ideal spot for a special and memorable experience. We have taken the rich history and tradition of fondue, combined it with modern touches and an intimate setting, and paired it with the perfect wines to provide you, our guest, with the most extraordinary dining experience anywhere.

It is our privilege to ensure that guests at The Melting Pot have the opportunity to dip into something different every time they visit. We have an extensive four-course menu, including cheese fondue, gourmet salads, entrée fondue, and our special chocolate dessert fondue. Our cheese fondues are the perfect start to any meal. We use delicate blends of Gruyère, Emmenthaler, Cheddar, and Blue cheese, among others, to create our distinctive first course, and we serve them with bread, apples, and fresh vegetables. We also have a wide variety of main course options, including a choice of four flavorful fondue cooking styles and a variety of tasty entrées, including premium cuts of beef, boneless breast of chicken, duck, lobster, shrimp, scallops, salmon, and much more. All the entrée choices are available in many combinations with a variety of special dipping sauces. Savory vegetables and a choice of several fresh salads accompany each entrée. And, of course, what meal would be complete without dessert? We guarantee that you'll love The Melting Pot's wide selection of creamy, decadent chocolate fondues.

We are pleased to say that with more than 132 locations across the nation, The Melting Pot Restaurants is the country's largest fondue restaurant franchise and that, with your support, we are growing every day.

The Melting Pot Family

Now we are very proud to present our first cookbook, a chance for you to bring The Melting Pot into your home with each of these fondue recipes our chefs have created. We believe that the experience of sharing a special meal from a communal pot with friends and family is what makes fondue unique, and we hope that you will use this cookbook to share many special fondue moments with those you love.

Table of Contents

A Dip into the Past
The History of Fondue

Fondue gets its name from the French verb *fondre*, which means "to melt." Most people think of fondue as a thick cheese mixture used for dipping, but The Melting Pot takes this simple dish to a gourmet level by combining fondue in its most traditional form with tasty modern twists.

Fondue, most experts agree, has its origins high in the mountains of Switzerland, where Swiss cow herders melted down their hardened cheese on cold nights. The herders, who were up in the mountains for long periods of time, were usually provisioned with foods that wouldn't spoil, including hard cheeses, loaves of bread, and bottles of wine. As time went by and provisions became stale, the herders would melt the cheese in their *caquelons* (earthenware cooking pots) over the fire, stir in a little wine, and dip the hardened bread into it. This simple but tasty dish eventually made its way into the homes of Swiss nobility by way of peasant kitchen servants.

No one is entirely certain how this traditional Swiss dish came to be associated with French cuisine, but it would seem that these Swiss nobles often served fondue while entertaining visitors from neighboring countries— including Austria, Liechtenstein, Italy, Germany, and, of course, France. The French, who have long been known for their love of all things culinary, christened the dish "fondue" and so it has been ever since.

The French people adopted the dish with gusto, but fondue didn't make its way to America until the late 1790s, when French gastronome and musician Jean Brillat-Savarin fled to Boston to escape the French Revolution. He introduced Americans to a number of French delicacies, including *fondue au fromage*. However, Americans didn't embrace fondue whole-heartedly until the late 1950s, when affluent American tourists began to flock to the Swiss Alps to ski. These international travelers brought their hunger for fondue back home, and classic Swiss cheese fondue became popular everywhere, from New York's finest restaurants to California dinner parties.

10

Fondue really came into its own, however, in 1956, when New York's Swiss Chalet restaurant introduced Fondue Bourguignonne, a style of fondue in which cubes of meat are cooked in a communal pot of hot oil. Fondue became more popular yet when Swiss Chalet debuted chocolate dessert fondue in 1964. Fondue remained in vogue as the most popular party food across America throughout the 1960s and into the 1970s. As time passed, fondue became less a trendy dish and more of an American mainstay, but it never lost its appeal. Still popular today, it is always a hit at special occasions and parties.

Different forms of this versatile dish have developed all over the world, each one as unique as its country of origin. Fondue Orientale, a method of cooking cubes of meat and vegetables in broth, was used in Mongolia as early as the fourteenth century. The Shabu-Shabu of Japan is a mildly seasoned broth; their Maotu is a spicy Szechwan broth. Both are used for cooking meat in a communal pot. Spain and Italy favor their Bourguignonne-style dishes—Spain's is called El Gran Frou Frou and Italy's is Fritto Misto. Even in Switzerland, where cheese fondue reigns supreme, there is a traditional broth fondue called Fondue Chinoise. And in Wales, Cheddar cheese fondue came to be known as Welsh Rabbit, since peasant women often prepared it when their husbands returned empty-handed from a hunting trip.

Fondue has come a long way since its humble beginnings. It has evolved from a peasant dish into a delicacy that has been influenced by tastes from around the globe. But one thing is certain: Fondue in all its delectable forms has found its ultimate home at The Melting Pot.

A Dip into Something Special
The History of The Melting Pot

In April of 1975, best friends Bruce Knoechel and Roy Nelson opened a small fondue restaurant in Maitland, Florida, just outside Orlando. They called it The Melting Pot. The cozy, intimate restaurant served only four dishes and two salads: Swiss cheese fondue, beef and chicken fondue Bourguignonne, milk chocolate fondue, the chef salad, and the mushroom salad. It was the seventies, and fondue was really taking off in America, and their little restaurant was a hit. Business was booming and they needed help, so they hired several eager college students to help wait tables.

One of those students was Mark Johnston, who worked as a waiter and assistant manager while he attended college. He loved The Melting Pot concept and believed it would be just as popular in other locations. After graduation, Mark convinced his brother Mike to go into business with him. They opened the third Melting Pot in Tallahassee in 1979, with the blessing of the original owners, of course. Their younger brother, Bob, joined them in 1979 as a dishwasher in the Tallahassee location. This restaurant was an instant hit, too, and in 1981 the two Johnston brothers opened another one in Tampa. Business was booming, and the brothers saw more opportunities to expand—but they didn't want to spread themselves too thin. The answer was simple: They needed to open more franchises.

In 1985, Bob joined his two brothers in partnership and the Johnstons established The Melting Pot Restaurants, Inc., when they bought the rights to The Melting Pot brand from their old friends Bruce and Roy. After a year of planning, organizing, and restructuring, The Melting Pot Restaurants, Inc., began searching for dedicated and energetic potential franchise owners. The brothers chose well and over the years have managed to build a close-knit fondue family. Today, with more than 132 locations across the country and thirty-two in development, The Melting Pot Restaurants, Inc., is the country's largest and most successful fondue restaurant franchise.

The Johnston brothers are still the heart and soul of The Melting Pot. Mark, the chief executive officer, is responsible for the overall growth and expansion of more than 132 Melting Pot locations across America, including site selection, lease negotiations, new restaurant development and design, and new concept creation.

Robert Johnston, the president and chief operating officer, oversees the daily operation of all the locations, strategic growth plans, recruiting and managing the executive leadership team, managing the company's fiscal and marketing strategies, and corporate partnerships. Mike continues to operate their first location in Tallahassee, while providing guidance and support to his brothers. The Johnstons are firm believers in giving back to the communities that support their business, and The Melting Pot Restaurants, Inc., partnered nationally with St. Jude Children's Research Hospital in 2002 to share the success The Melting Pot enjoys and give back to those in need. They encourage their franchisees to give locally to charities in need in addition to raising money annually for St. Jude. In Tampa, Florida, where the home office is based, they provide charitable support to more than forty local and regional civic organizations and charities. It is simply one of their commitments reflected in the company's culture and principles. The nine principles that guide every decision this organization makes are pride, quality, leadership, accountability, teamwork, learning, hospitality, family and belonging, and integrity. They believe their success is wholly based on their commitment to these nine core principles.

The future looks bright for fondue and The Melting Pot Restaurants, Inc., thanks to the company's dedication to innovation, quality, and impeccable service. For more than three decades, The Melting Pot has defined the fondue niche across the American dining scene, and, with your support, it will continue to do so for many years to come.

The Golden Appeal

of a Cheese Fondue

At The Melting Pot, we have a soft spot for cheese fondue. It's one of our signature dishes because, of course, like so many people, we love rich, warm, melted cheese.

The great cheeses of the world can become great fondues on your table. Fondue had its beginnings as a hearty peasant food of the Alpine Swiss but is now well known and made all over the world. It began with Switzerland's local cheeses — Emmenthaler and Gruyère — but you can experiment with other great cheeses of the world: Goudas and Edams from the Netherlands; Asiagos and Parmigiano-Reggianos from Italy; crumbly Blues from France; flavorful Manchegos from Spain; and tangy Feta from Greece. Combined with beer, wine, or broth and flavored with herbs and seasonings, each cheese becomes a different dreamy fondue.

In this section, you'll find recipes for some of your Melting Pot cheese fondue favorites, including Traditional Swiss, Zesty Cheddar, and Wisconsin Trio. We've also included recipes for some of our rotating seasonal specialties and a few new cheese fondues that are sure to be a hit. Grab your favorite vegetables and breads for dipping, and give each of these tasty cheese fondues a try.

Step-by-Step Cheese Fondue

Follow these simple steps for making a great pot of cheese fondue.

1. Slowly pour liquid, such as wine or broth, into the top of a double boiler or a metal bowl set over a saucepan of simmering water.

2. Stir in lemon juice and garlic using a fork. Cook for 30 seconds, stirring constantly.

3. Add half the amount of cheese called for in the recipe.

Step 1

Step 2

Step 3

4. Cook until the cheese is melted, stirring constantly.

5. Add the remaining cheese a small amount at a time, stirring constantly in a circular motion after each addition until the cheese is melted. The fondue should be the consistency of warm honey when completed. Monitor the cheese carefully as it is being added. Not all of the cheese may be needed, and, in some cases, more cheese may be needed to reach the perfect consistency.

6. Stir in any seasonings called for in the recipe.

Step 4

Step 5

Step 6

Wisconsin Trio Fondue

1 1/2 cups (6 ounces) shredded
  Butterkäse
1 1/2 cups (6 ounces) shredded
  Fontina cheese
3 tablespoons all-purpose flour
3/4 cup white wine
1/4 cup dry sherry
2 teaspoons chopped shallots
1 teaspoon freshly ground pepper
1/4 cup crumbled Blue cheese
2 tablespoons chopped scallions

Serves 4 to 6

Toss the Butterkäse and Fontina cheese with the flour in a bowl. Place a metal bowl over a saucepan filled with 2 inches of water. You may also use a conventional double boiler. Bring the water to a boil over high heat. Reduce the heat to medium and pour the wine and sherry into the bowl. Stir in the shallots using a fork. Cook for 30 seconds, stirring constantly.

Add half the cheese blend and cook until the cheese is melted, stirring constantly. Add the remaining cheese blend a small amount at a time, stirring constantly in a circular motion after each addition until the cheese is melted. Fold in the pepper and Blue cheese. Pour into a warm fondue pot and keep warm over low heat. Garnish with the scallions.

Note—The cheese is shredded and tossed with flour to aid in thickening and to improve the viscosity of the fondue. The fondue should be the consistency of warm honey when completed. Monitor the cheese carefully as it is being added. Not all of the cheese may be needed, and, in some cases, more cheese may be needed to reach the perfect consistency.

Fondue Pomodoro

2³/4 cups (11 ounces) shredded
    Cheddar cheese
3 tablespoons all-purpose flour
³/4 cup beer (light beer
    recommended)
¹/4 cup chunky tomato sauce
4 teaspoons finely chopped garlic
2 tablespoons basil pesto
1 teaspoon freshly ground pepper

Serves 4 to 6

Toss the cheese with the flour in a bowl. Place a metal bowl over a saucepan filled with 2 inches of water. You may also use a conventional double boiler. Bring the water to a boil over high heat. Reduce the heat to medium and pour the beer and tomato sauce into the bowl. Stir in the garlic and pesto using a fork. Cook for 30 seconds, stirring constantly.

Add half the cheese and cook until the cheese is melted, stirring constantly. Add the remaining cheese a small amount at a time, stirring constantly in a circular motion after each addition until the cheese is melted. Stir in the pepper. Pour into a warm fondue pot and keep warm over low heat.

Note—The cheese is shredded and tossed with flour to aid in thickening and to improve the viscosity of the fondue. The fondue should be the consistency of warm honey when completed. Monitor the cheese carefully as it is being added. Not all the cheese may be needed, and, in some cases, more cheese may be needed to reach the perfect consistency.

Garlic and Herb Cheddar Fondue

2³/₄ cups (11 ounces) shredded
    Cheddar cheese
3 tablespoons all-purpose flour
1 cup beer (light beer recommended)
4 teaspoons chopped garlic
6 tablespoons Green Goddess
    Sauce (page 104)
1 teaspoon The Melting Pot Garlic
    and Wine Seasoning (optional)
1 teaspoon freshly ground pepper

Serves 4 to 6

Toss the cheese with the flour in a bowl. Place a metal bowl over a saucepan filled with 2 inches of water. You may also use a conventional double boiler. Bring the water to a boil over high heat. Reduce the heat to medium and pour the beer into the bowl. Stir in the garlic using a fork. Cook for 30 seconds, stirring constantly.

Add half the cheese and cook until the cheese is melted, stirring constantly. Add the remaining cheese a small amount at a time, stirring constantly in a circular motion after each addition until the cheese is melted. Fold in the Green Goddess Sauce, Garlic and Wine Seasoning and pepper. Pour into a warm fondue pot and keep warm over low heat.

Note—The cheese is shredded and tossed with flour to aid in thickening and to improve the viscosity of the fondue. The fondue should be the consistency of warm honey when completed. Monitor the cheese carefully as it is being added. Not all the cheese may be needed, and, in some cases, more cheese may be needed to reach the perfect consistency.

Fondue Myths and Legends

A funny, but common, fondue myth is that cheese fondue will harden in your stomach if you drink a cold beverage while eating it. Some people even go so far as to claim that this is why it's customary to serve red wine kept at room temperature with cheese fondue. This story is certainly not true, but it is a great icebreaker at fondue parties.

21

Cranberry Cheddar Fondue

2³/4 cups (11 ounces) shredded
    Cheddar cheese
3 tablespoons all-purpose flour
1 cup hard cider (Strongbow brand
    recommended)
2 teaspoons finely chopped shallots
2 teaspoons dry mustard
2 tablespoons chopped sweetened
    dried cranberries
1 teaspoon freshly ground pepper
2 teaspoons crushed walnuts

Serves 4 to 6

Toss the cheese with the flour in a bowl. Place a metal bowl over a saucepan filled with 2 inches of water. You may also use a conventional double boiler. Bring the water to a boil over high heat. Reduce the heat to medium and pour the hard cider into the bowl. Stir in the shallots, mustard and cranberries using a fork. Cook for 30 seconds, stirring constantly.

Add half the cheese and cook until the cheese is melted, stirring constantly. Add the remaining cheese a small amount at a time, stirring constantly in a circular motion after each addition until the cheese is melted. Stir in the pepper. Pour into a warm fondue pot and keep warm over low heat. Garnish with the walnuts.

Note—The cheese is shredded and tossed with flour to aid in thickening and to improve the viscosity of the fondue. The fondue should be the consistency of warm honey when completed. Monitor the cheese carefully as it is being added. Not all the cheese may be needed, and, in some cases, more cheese may be needed to reach the perfect consistency.

Voodoo Cheddar Fondue

2³/₄ cups (11 ounces) shredded
   Cheddar cheese
3 tablespoons all-purpose flour
1 cup beer (light beer recommended)
¹/₂ cup diced tomatoes with
   green chiles
2 teaspoons finely chopped garlic
¹/₂ cup cooked baby shrimp
1 teaspoon freshly ground pepper

Serves 4 to 6

Toss the cheese with the flour in a bowl. Place a metal bowl over a saucepan filled with 2 inches of water. You may also use a conventional double boiler. Bring the water to a boil over high heat. Reduce the heat to medium and pour the beer into the bowl. Stir in the tomatoes with green chiles and garlic using a fork. Cook for 30 seconds, stirring constantly.

Add half the cheese and cook until the cheese is melted, stirring constantly. Add the remaining cheese a small amount at a time, stirring constantly in a circular motion after each addition until the cheese is melted. Fold in the shrimp and pepper. Pour into a warm fondue pot and keep warm over low heat.

Note—The cheese is shredded and tossed with flour to aid in thickening and to improve the viscosity of the fondue. The fondue should be the consistency of warm honey when completed. Monitor the cheese carefully as it is being added. Not all the cheese may be needed, and, in some cases, more cheese may be needed to reach the perfect consistency.

Zesty Cheddar Fondue

2¾ cups (11 ounces) shredded
    Cheddar cheese
3 tablespoons all-purpose flour
1 cup beer (light beer recommended)
4 teaspoons prepared horseradish
2 teaspoons Worcestershire sauce
4 teaspoons dry mustard
2 tablespoons chopped cooked
    bacon
2 teaspoons freshly ground pepper
1 tablespoon chopped scallions

Serves 4 to 6

Toss the cheese with the flour in a bowl. Place a metal bowl over a saucepan filled with 2 inches of water. You may also use a conventional double boiler. Bring the water to a boil over high heat. Reduce the heat to medium and pour the beer into the bowl. Press the liquid from the horseradish. Stir the horseradish, Worcestershire sauce and mustard into the beer using a fork. Cook for 30 seconds, stirring constantly.

Add half the cheese and cook until the cheese is melted, stirring constantly. Add the remaining cheese a small amount at a time, stirring constantly in a circular motion after each addition until the cheese is melted. Fold in the bacon and pepper. Pour into a warm fondue pot and keep warm over low heat. Garnish with the scallions.

Note—The cheese is shredded and tossed with flour to aid in thickening and to improve the viscosity of the fondue. The fondue should be the consistency of warm honey when completed. Monitor the cheese carefully as it is being added. Not all the cheese may be needed, and, in some cases, more cheese may be needed to reach the perfect consistency.

 ## Types of Cheese—Cheddar

Cheddar cheese is a hard cheese that ranges in color from very pale yellow to bright orange and in taste from quite mild to very sharp. Cheddar cheese originated in the English village of Cheddar, in Somerset, but is now produced all over the world. It is one of the most popular and versatile types of cheese and can be found in almost any supermarket. A high-quality lager beer makes a nice base for Cheddar cheese fondue.

Broccoli and Cheddar Fondue

2³/4 cups (11 ounces) shredded
    Cheddar cheese
3 tablespoons all-purpose flour
1 cup beer (light beer recommended)
2 teaspoons finely chopped garlic
2 teaspoons finely chopped shallots
1¹/2 cups chopped fresh broccoli
2 teaspoons freshly ground pepper

Serves 4 to 6

Toss the cheese with the flour in a bowl. Place a metal bowl over a saucepan filled with 2 inches of water. You may also use a conventional double boiler. Bring the water to a boil over high heat. Reduce the heat to medium and pour the beer into the bowl. Stir in the garlic and shallots using a fork. Cook for 30 seconds, stirring constantly.

Add half the cheese and cook until the cheese is melted, stirring constantly. Add the remaining cheese a small amount at a time, stirring constantly in a circular motion after each addition until the cheese is melted. Fold in the broccoli and pepper. Pour into a warm fondue pot and keep warm over low heat.

 Fondue Cooking Tips

Do not add water to cheese fondue. If it is too thick, add more of the liquid you used for the base. If it is too thin, add more cheese.

Keep the heat as low as possible so that the cheese doesn't become rubbery.

Wondering what to drink with your cheese fondue? Try more of the wine or beer you used as the base in the recipe!

When cooking using the Fondue Bourguignonne Cooking Style (page 84), too many fondue forks in the pot at one time will lower the temperature of the oil and cause the meat to cook improperly.

Note—The cheese is shredded and tossed with flour to aid in thickening and to improve the viscosity of the fondue. The fondue should be the consistency of warm honey when completed. Monitor the cheese carefully as it is being added. Not all the cheese may be needed, and, in some cases, more cheese may be needed to reach the perfect consistency.

Chicken Club Fondue

2¾ cups (11 ounces) shredded
    Cheddar cheese
3 tablespoons all-purpose flour
½ cup beer (light beer recommended)
½ cup low-sodium chicken broth
½ cup finely chopped cooked
    chicken
½ cup finely chopped tomato
¼ cup chopped cooked bacon
2 tablespoons mayonnaise
2 tablespoons chopped scallions

Serves 4 to 6

Toss the cheese with the flour in a bowl. Place a metal bowl over a saucepan filled with 2 inches of water. You may also use a conventional double boiler. Bring the water to a boil over high heat. Reduce the heat to medium and pour the beer and broth into the bowl. Cook for 30 seconds, stirring constantly.

Add half the cheese and cook until the cheese is melted, stirring constantly. Add the remaining cheese a small amount at a time, stirring constantly in a circular motion after each addition until the cheese is melted. Fold in the chicken, tomato and bacon. Stir in the mayonnaise. Pour into a warm fondue pot and keep warm over low heat. Garnish with the scallions.

Note—The cheese is shredded and tossed with flour to aid in thickening and to improve the viscosity of the fondue. The fondue should be the consistency of warm honey when completed. Monitor the cheese carefully as it is being added. Not all the cheese may be needed, and, in some cases, more cheese may be needed to reach the perfect consistency.

27

Bourbon Bacon Cheddar Fondue

2³/₄ cups (11 ounces) shredded
    Cheddar cheese
3 tablespoons all-purpose flour
1 cup beer (light beer
    recommended)
4 teaspoons prepared horseradish
4 teaspoons dry mustard
2 teaspoons Worcestershire sauce
1 tablespoon bourbon
2 tablespoons chopped cooked
    bacon
2 teaspoons freshly ground pepper
4 teaspoons chopped scallions

Serves 4 to 6

Toss the cheese with the flour in a bowl. Place a metal bowl over a saucepan filled with 2 inches of water. You may also use a conventional double boiler. Bring the water to a boil over high heat. Reduce the heat to medium and pour the beer into the bowl. Stir in the horseradish, mustard and Worcestershire sauce using a fork. Cook for 30 seconds, stirring constantly.

Add half the cheese and cook until the cheese is melted, stirring constantly. Add the remaining cheese a small amount at a time, stirring constantly in a circular motion after each addition until the cheese is melted. Pour the bourbon slowly around the edge of the bowl. Pull the cheese mixture away from the edge of the bowl and cook for about 30 seconds or until the alcohol cooks off. Stir the bourbon into the cheese. Fold in the bacon and pepper. Pour into a warm fondue pot and keep warm over low heat. Garnish with the scallions.

Note—The cheese is shredded and tossed with flour to aid in thickening and to improve the viscosity of the fondue. The fondue should be the consistency of warm honey when completed. Monitor the cheese carefully as it is being added. Not all the cheese may be needed, and, in some cases, more cheese may be needed to reach the perfect consistency.

Fun Fondue Fork-lore— la Courte

Cheese fondue is so delicious that the pot is usually empty all too soon. But there is treasure to be found at the end of the cheese fondue course. The hard crust of cheese left at the bottom is called "la courte" or "la religuese" and is considered a delicacy in Switzerland and France. So remove this delicacy, cut it into pieces, and enjoy!

French Onion Swiss Fondue

3¹/2 cups (14 ounces) shredded
　　Swiss cheese
2 tablespoons all-purpose flour
1 cup beef stock, prepared using
　　Minor's beef base
¹/2 cup Onion Relish (below)
2 teaspoons finely chopped garlic
¹/4 teaspoon Worcestershire sauce
2 teaspoons freshly ground pepper
2 tablespoons chopped scallions

Serves 4 to 6

Toss the cheese with the flour in a bowl. Place a metal bowl over a saucepan filled with 2 inches of water. You may also use a conventional double boiler. Bring the water to a boil over high heat. Reduce the heat to medium and pour the stock into the bowl. Stir in the Onion Relish and garlic using a fork. Cook for 30 seconds, stirring constantly.

Add half the cheese and cook until the cheese is melted, stirring constantly. Add the remaining cheese a small amount at a time, stirring constantly in a circular motion after each addition until the cheese is melted. Stir the Worcestershire sauce and pepper in gently. Pour into a warm fondue pot and keep warm over low heat. Garnish with the scallions.

Note—The cheese is shredded and tossed with flour to aid in thickening and to improve the viscosity of the fondue. The fondue should be the consistency of warm honey when completed. Monitor the cheese carefully as it is being added. Not all the cheese may be needed, and, in some cases, more cheese may be needed to reach the perfect consistency.

Onion Relish

1 cup finely chopped white onion
1 teaspoon chopped garlic
1 tablespoon butter
1 cup red wine

Makes about 1 cup

Sauté the onion and garlic in the butter in a sauté pan over medium heat until the onion is translucent. Add the red wine and cook until most of the liquid has evaporated, stirring frequently. Pour into a bowl and chill, covered, for 30 minutes or longer.

Smoked Salmon and Vodka Fondue

3 cups (12 ounces) shredded
   Swiss cheese
3 tablespoons all-purpose flour
1 cup white wine
4 teaspoons finely chopped garlic
1/4 cup Green Goddess Sauce
   (page 104)
1/2 cup chopped smoked salmon
1 1/2 tablespoons vodka
2 teaspoons capers
2 tablespoons chopped scallions

Serves 4 to 6

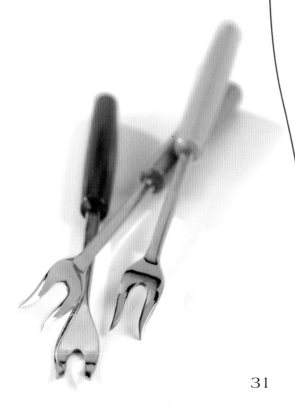

Toss the cheese with the flour in a bowl. Place a metal bowl over a saucepan filled with 2 inches of water. You may also use a conventional double boiler. Bring the water to a boil over high heat. Reduce the heat to medium and pour the wine into the bowl. Stir in the garlic, Green Goddess Sauce and salmon using a fork. Cook for 30 seconds, stirring constantly.

Add half the cheese and cook until the cheese is melted, stirring constantly. Add the remaining cheese a small amount at a time, stirring constantly in a circular motion after each addition until the cheese is melted. Pour the vodka in slowly around the edge of the bowl. Pull the cheese mixture away from the edge of the bowl and cook for about 30 seconds or until the alcohol cooks off. Fold the capers in gently. Pour into a warm fondue pot and keep warm over low heat. Garnish with the scallions.

Note—The cheese is shredded and tossed with flour to aid in thickening and to improve the viscosity of the fondue. The fondue should be the consistency of warm honey when completed. Monitor the cheese carefully as it is being added. Not all the cheese may be needed, and, in some cases, more cheese may be needed to reach the perfect consistency.

Traditional Swiss Fondue

3 1/2 cups (14 ounces) shredded
    Swiss cheese
2 tablespoons all-purpose flour
1 cup white wine
2 tablespoons fresh lemon juice
2 teaspoons finely chopped garlic
1 ounce cherry-flavored liqueur
    (Kirschwasser recommended)
1/2 teaspoon freshly ground pepper
Dash of grated nutmeg

Serves 4 to 6

Note—The cheese is shredded and tossed with flour to aid in thickening and to improve the viscosity of the fondue. The fondue should be the consistency of warm honey when completed. Monitor the cheese carefully as it is being added. Not all the cheese may be needed, and, in some cases, more cheese may be needed to reach the perfect consistency.

Toss the cheese with the flour in a bowl. Place a metal bowl over a saucepan filled with 2 inches of water. You may also use a conventional double boiler. Bring the water to a boil over high heat. Reduce the heat to medium and pour the wine into the bowl. Stir in the lemon juice and garlic using a fork. Cook for 30 seconds, stirring constantly. Add half the cheese and cook until the cheese is melted, stirring constantly. Add the remaining cheese a small amount at a time, stirring constantly in a circular motion after each addition until the cheese is melted. Pour the liqueur slowly around the edge of the bowl. Pull the cheese mixture away from the edge of the bowl and cook for about 1 minute or until the alcohol cooks off. Stir the liqueur into the cheese. Stir the pepper in gently. Pour into a warm fondue pot and keep warm over low heat. Garnish with a dash of nutmeg.

 ## Types of Cheese—Swiss

Two of the most well-known cheeses come from Switzerland and are also two of the most popular fondue cheeses. Emmenthaler has a slight piquant flavor but is not particularly sharp. It is a medium-hard, yellow cheese and is famous for its large holes. Gruyère is a harder yellow cheese made from cow's milk and named after the town of Gruyère. Gruyère has a sweet but slightly salty flavor that becomes more complex with age. It is creamier with a nuttier taste when young, but as it ages, it develops a more aggressive and earthier flavor. White wine or Champagne makes a great base for Swiss cheese fondue.

Feta and Walnut Fondue

¹/₄ cup (¹/₂ stick) unsalted butter
2 tablespoons all-purpose flour
2 cups milk
³/₄ cup to 1 cup Feta cheese
1 tablespoon chopped scallions
1 tablespoon chopped parsley
Kosher salt to taste
Freshly ground pepper to taste
¹/₄ cup finely chopped
    toasted walnuts

Serves 4 to 6

Melt the butter in a 2-quart saucepan over medium heat. Stir in the flour using a wooden spoon. Heat until the mixture forms a smooth paste, stirring constantly. Whisk in the milk. Reduce the heat and simmer for 10 minutes or until the mixture thickens, stirring constantly. Fold in the cheese, scallions and parsley. Season with salt and pepper. Pour into a warm fondue pot and keep warm over low heat. Garnish with the walnuts. Serve with dippers of melon, pitted olives or sliced prosciutto in addition to your favorite breads and vegetables.

Creamy Garlic and Herb Cheese Fondue

1 1/2 teaspoons finely chopped
   fresh thyme
1 teaspoon finely chopped garlic
1 tablespoon unsalted butter
2 cups heavy cream
8 ounces Cambozola cheese or Brie
   cheese, finely chopped
1/4 teaspoon freshly ground pepper

Serves 4 to 6

Cook the thyme and garlic in the butter in a small saucepan over medium-low heat for 2 minutes or until the garlic is soft; do not brown the garlic. Add the cream and increase the heat to medium-high. Bring to a simmer. Decrease the heat and simmer until the cream is reduced by one-third, stirring frequently. Stir in the cheese using a fork. Cook until the cheese is melted, stirring constantly. Stir in the pepper. Pour into a warm fondue pot and keep warm over low heat.

Note—You may make this sauce a couple of hours in advance, but it should be reheated very slowly to prevent separation. A number of cheeses can be substituted for the Cambozola—try Brie cheese, Blue cheese, or aged English Cheddar cheese. Alternatively, use this sauce as a base for lasagna, tossed with pasta and steamed asparagus, or spoon over grilled steak for a stunning accent.

 ## Types of Cheese— Blue Cheese

Blue Cheese is a general classification of cow's milk, sheep's milk, or goat's milk cheese that has had certain types of *penicillium* cultures added so that the final product is veined or spotted throughout with blue or blue-green mold. Blue cheeses are characterized by their sharp and slightly salty flavors, as well as their pungent odors. Blue cheeses are easily crumbled and make very rich, flavorful fondues.

Chipotle Swiss Fondue

3¹/₂ cups (14 ounces) shredded
    Swiss cheese
2 tablespoons all-purpose flour
1 cup white wine
2 teaspoons finely chopped garlic
4 teaspoons finely chopped
    chipotle chile
2 tablespoons chopped
    cooked bacon
1 teaspoon freshly ground pepper
1 tablespoon chopped scallions

    Serves 4 to 6

Toss the cheese with the flour in a bowl. Place a metal bowl over a saucepan filled with 2 inches of water. You may also use a conventional double boiler. Bring the water to a boil over high heat. Reduce the heat to medium and pour the wine into the bowl. Stir in the garlic using a fork. Cook for 30 seconds, stirring constantly.

Add half the cheese and cook until the cheese is melted, stirring constantly. Add the remaining cheese a small amount at a time, stirring constantly in a circular motion after each addition until the cheese is melted. Fold in the chile, bacon and pepper. Pour into a warm fondue pot and keep warm over low heat. Garnish with the scallions.

Note—The cheese is shredded and tossed with flour to aid in thickening and to improve the viscosity of the fondue. The fondue should be the consistency of warm honey when completed. Monitor the cheese carefully as it is being added. Not all the cheese may be needed, and, in some cases, more cheese may be needed to reach the perfect consistency.

 Fondue Myths and Legends

There is a French legend that says cheese fondue can be ruined by something as simple as stirring. According to the legend, cheese fondue must be stirred consistently either clockwise or counterclockwise while it is being prepared. But once you begin stirring one way, you cannot switch to stir in the opposite direction or the fondue will be ruined. Luckily, we haven't ruined a pot yet by stirring the cheese the wrong way!

Feng Shui Fondue

1 1/2 cups (6 ounces) shredded
　　Butterkäse
1 1/2 cups (6 ounces) shredded
　　Fontina cheese
3 tablespoons all-purpose flour
1/2 cup white wine
1/4 cup dry sake
1/4 cup rice wine
2 teaspoons finely chopped garlic
2 teaspoons finely chopped shallots
2 teaspoons crushed red pepper
2 tablespoons chopped scallions

Serves 4 to 6

Toss the Butterkäse and Fontina cheese with the flour in a bowl. Place a metal bowl over a saucepan filled with 2 inches of water. You may also use a conventional double boiler. Bring the water to a boil over high heat. Reduce the heat to medium and pour the white wine, sake and rice wine into the bowl. Stir in the garlic, shallots and red pepper using a fork. Cook for 30 seconds, stirring constantly.

Add half the cheese blend and cook until the cheese is melted, stirring constantly. Add the remaining cheese blend a small amount at a time, stirring constantly in a circular motion after each addition until the cheese is melted. Pour into a warm fondue pot and keep warm over low heat. Garnish with the scallions.

Note—The cheese is shredded and tossed with flour to aid in thickening and to improve the viscosity of the fondue. The fondue should be the consistency of warm honey when completed. Monitor the cheese carefully as it is being added. Not all the cheese may be needed, and, in some cases, more cheese may be needed to reach the perfect consistency.

Types of Cheese— Butterkäse

Butterkäse is a creamy, semi-soft cheese that is made in both Germany and Austria. It can range in color from pale gold to pale red and has a buttery, delicate flavor. It melts beautifully, and its mild flavor makes it an ideal candidate for blending with other cheeses to create a fondue with layers of different tastes. White wine makes the best base for Butterkäse fondue, but a light vegetable broth also works well.

Goat Cheese Fondue

1/2 cup white wine

1/4 cup sherry

2 tablespoons fresh orange juice

2 tablespoons finely chopped shallots

1 (5-ounce) round Boursin cheese

1/4 cup goat cheese

1/4 cup Humboldt Fog aged
   goat cheese

1 cup (4 ounces) shredded
   Swiss cheese

1/4 cup sliced toasted almonds

Serves 4 to 6

Place a metal bowl over a saucepan filled with 2 inches of water. You may also use a conventional double boiler. Bring the water to a boil over high heat. Reduce the heat to medium and pour the wine and sherry into the bowl. Stir in the orange juice and shallots using a fork. Cook for 30 seconds, stirring constantly.

Add the Boursin cheese, goat cheese, Humboldt Fog goat cheese and Swiss cheese in the order listed, stirring after each addition until melted. Pour into a warm fondue pot and keep warm over low heat. Garnish with the almonds.

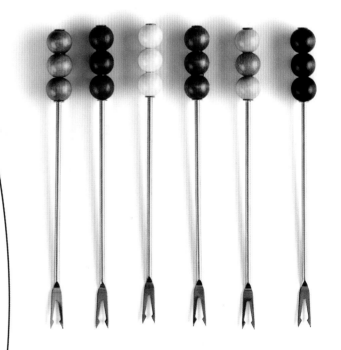

Macaroni and Four Cheese Fondue

1/2 cup (2 ounces) shredded
  Fontina cheese
1/2 cup (2 ounces) shredded sharp
  Cheddar cheese
1/2 cup (2 ounces) shredded
  Swiss cheese
1 tablespoon all-purpose flour
1/2 cup white wine
2 tablespoons sherry
1 tablespoon finely chopped garlic
1/2 cup cooked and cooled
  elbow macaroni
1 tablespoon crumbled
  Blue cheese

Serves 4 to 6

Toss the Fontina cheese, Cheddar cheese and Swiss cheese with the flour in a bowl. Place a metal bowl over a saucepan filled with 2 inches of water. You may also use a conventional double boiler. Bring the water to a boil over high heat. Reduce the heat to medium and pour the wine and sherry into the bowl. Stir in the garlic using a fork. Cook for 30 seconds, stirring constantly.

Add half the cheese blend and cook until the cheese is melted, stirring constantly. Add the remaining cheese blend a small amount at a time, stirring constantly in a circular motion after each addition until the cheese is melted. Fold in the pasta and Blue cheese gently. Pour into a warm fondue pot and keep warm over low heat.

Note—The cheese is shredded and tossed with flour to aid in thickening and to improve the viscosity of the fondue. The fondue should be the consistency of warm honey when completed. Monitor the cheese carefully as it is being added. Not all the cheese may be needed, and, in some cases, more cheese may be needed to reach the perfect consistency.

Types of Cheese—Fontina

Fontina cheese is an Italian cow's milk cheese that has been made in the Alps since the 12th century. Young Fontina cheese has a softer texture and a slightly nutty, mild taste. Mature Fontina cheese is a hard, rich cheese with a slightly fruity flavor. Young Fontina cheese melts extremely well, which makes it an ideal cheese for fondue. The light flavor of Fontina cheese is best showcased when mixed with a white wine as a base.

Red Pepper Stilton Fondue

1¹/₂ cups (6 ounces) shredded
  Butterkäse
1¹/₂ cups (6 ounces) shredded
  Fontina cheese
3 tablespoons all-purpose flour
³/₄ cup white wine
¹/₄ cup sherry
¹/₄ cup finely chopped roasted
  red pepper
2 tablespoons finely chopped
  shallots
6 tablespoons crumbled Stilton
  cheese or other Blue cheese

Serves 4 to 6

Toss the Butterkäse and Fontina cheese with the flour in a bowl. Place a metal bowl over a saucepan filled with 2 inches of water. You may also use a conventional double boiler. Bring the water to a boil over high heat. Reduce the heat to medium and pour the wine and sherry into the bowl. Stir in the red pepper and shallots using a fork. Cook for 30 seconds, stirring constantly.

Add half the cheese blend and cook until the cheese is melted, stirring constantly. Add the remaining cheese blend a small amount at a time, stirring constantly in a circular motion after each addition until the cheese is melted. Fold in the Stilton cheese gently. Pour into a warm fondue pot and keep warm over low heat.

Note—The cheese is shredded and tossed with flour to aid in thickening and to improve the viscosity of the fondue. The fondue should be the consistency of warm honey when completed. Monitor the cheese carefully as it is being added. Not all the cheese may be needed, and, in some cases, more cheese may be needed to reach the perfect consistency.

The Golden Appeal of a Cheese Fondue

Crab Meat and Brie Fondue

¹/₄ cup (¹/₂ stick) unsalted butter
¹/₂ cup finely chopped shallots
2 cups heavy cream
2 cups cubed Brie cheese
2 teaspoons kosher salt
1 teaspoon freshly ground pepper
1 pound lump crab meat, shells
   removed and meat flaked
2 tablespoons chopped
   fresh parsley

Serves 4 to 6

Heat the butter in a large skillet over medium heat. Add the shallots and sauté for 1 minute or until the shallots are translucent. Add the cream and bring to a simmer.

Whisk the Brie cheese into the cream mixture. Season with the salt and pepper. Stir in the crab meat. Cook for 3 to 5 minutes or until the mixture is slightly reduced. Pour into a warm fondue pot and keep warm over low heat. Garnish with the parsley.

Salads and Dressings

Crisp greens and colorful vegetables in homemade dressing — at The Melting Pot, we think it's the best way to complement a meal. Choose the classic crunch of our Caesar Salad, the earthy, full-bodied Spinach Mushroom Salad, the refreshing Strawberry Fields Salad, the bold flavors of the California Salad, or one of our seasonal specialties.

In your kitchen, salads can make a first course, or serve as an entrée. They can be meticulously assembled from hand-prepared ingredients or casually thrown together. With a variety of lettuces, greens, vegetables, and fruits, there are many salad combinations.

Then there's the dressing — silky oils, tangy vinegars, drizzles of citrus, sweet and tart vinaigrettes, and creamy yogurt-based blends. With so many options, there are salads for every season and every taste. We've included our favorite recipes, but feel free to mix it up.

Cherry Blossom Salad

4 cups mixed salad greens
1 cup sliced mushrooms
1/4 cup dried cherries
2 tablespoons pecan pieces
Raspberry Walnut Vinaigrette
(below)

Serves 2

Toss the salad greens and mushrooms together in a bowl. Divide equally between two salad plates. Sprinkle with the cherries and pecans. Drizzle with the desired amount of Raspberry Walnut Vinaigrette.

Raspberry Walnut Vinaigrette

1 cup raspberry jam
1/4 cup cold water
1 tablespoon apple cider vinegar
1 teaspoon walnut oil
Kosher salt to taste
Freshly ground pepper to taste
1/4 cup canola oil

Makes 1 1/2 cups

Combine the jam, water, vinegar, walnut oil, salt and pepper in a bowl and mix well. Add the canola oil slowly, whisking constantly until blended. Store the vinaigrette in a jar with a tight-fitting lid in the refrigerator for up to 3 weeks.

Mandarin Orange and Almond Salad

4 cups mixed salad greens
1 cup shredded red cabbage
14 mandarin orange segments
Asian Salad Dressing (below)
2 tablespoons sliced
    almonds, toasted

Serves 2

Toss the salad greens, cabbage, orange sections and the desired amount of Asian Salad Dressing together in a bowl. Divide equally between two salad plates. Sprinkle with the almonds.

Asian Salad Dressing

1/2 cup packed light brown sugar
1 1/2 teaspoons dry mustard
1/2 cup rice wine
1/2 cup soy sauce
1 tablespoon honey
1 tablespoon lemon juice
Kosher salt to taste
1 tablespoon sesame oil
1 1/2 cups peanut oil

Makes 3 cups

Combine the brown sugar, mustard, rice wine, soy sauce, honey, lemon juice and salt in a bowl and whisk until the sugar is dissolved. Add the sesame oil and peanut oil slowly, whisking constantly until blended. Store the dressing in a jar with a tight-fitting lid in the refrigerator for up to 3 weeks.

Melting Pot Products

Now you can get some of your favorite Melting Pot goodies to go! Guests can purchase The Melting Pot's famous Garlic and Wine Seasoning, House Salad Dressing, Raspberry Walnut Vinaigrette Salad Dressing, and Parmesan Italian Salad Dressing to enjoy at home. You can even buy chocolate fondue bars in dark, milk, and white chocolate!

Bittersweet Spinach Salad

4¹/₂ cups baby spinach leaves
6 slices Roma tomato
¹/₄ cup crumbled Blue cheese
2 tablespoons golden raisins
2 tablespoons candied pecans
¹/₄ cup sliced roasted red pepper
Balsamic Vinaigrette (below)

Serves 2

Mound equal amounts of the spinach on two salad plates. Arrange the tomato slices around the spinach. Sprinkle with the Blue cheese, raisins and pecans. Mound the red pepper neatly in the center of the spinach. Drizzle with the desired amount of Balsamic Vinaigrette.

Balsamic Vinaigrette

¹/₂ cup balsamic vinegar
2 tablespoons finely chopped garlic
1¹/₂ tablespoons light brown sugar
1 teaspoon Dijon mustard
1 teaspoon kosher salt
1 teaspoon freshly ground pepper
1¹/₂ cups extra-virgin olive oil
Water

Makes 2 cups

Combine the vinegar, garlic, brown sugar, Dijon mustard, salt and pepper in a bowl and whisk until blended. Add the olive oil slowly, whisking constantly until blended. You may add water to reach the desired consistency if the dressing is too thick. Store the vinaigrette in a jar with a tight-fitting lid in the refrigerator for up to 3 weeks.

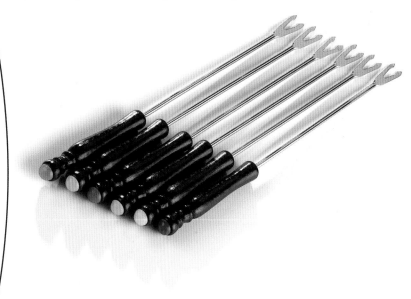

Strawberry Fields Salad

2 cups baby spinach leaves
2 cups mixed salad greens
1 cup sliced strawberries
1/4 cup crumbled Feta cheese
2 tablespoons sliced almonds,
   toasted
White Balsamic Vinaigrette (below)

Serves 2

Mound equal amounts of the spinach on two salad plates. Top with the salad greens. Sprinkle with the strawberries, cheese and almonds. Drizzle with the desired amount of White Balsamic Vinaigrette.

White Balsamic Vinaigrette

1 cup white balsamic vinegar
2 tablespoons sugar
1/4 cup minced shallots
1 tablespoon minced garlic
1 tablespoon Dijon mustard
2 teaspoons freshly ground pepper
2 cups vegetable oil

Makes 3 1/2 cups

Combine the vinegar, sugar, shallots, garlic, Dijon mustard and pepper in a bowl and mix well. Add the oil slowly, whisking constantly until blended. Store the vinaigrette in a jar with a tight-fitting lid in the refrigerator for up to 3 weeks.

Salads and Dressings

Belgian Endive Salad

4 cups mixed salad greens
6 slices Roma tomato
10 Belgian endive leaves
1/2 cup thinly sliced red onion
1/4 cup thinly sliced button
    mushrooms
Sweet Mustard Dressing (below)

Serves 2

Mound equal amounts of the salad greens on two salad plates. Arrange the tomatoes around the salad greens. Arrange five of the endive leaves in a star-shaped pattern over each salad. Sprinkle with the onion and mushrooms. Drizzle with the desired amount of Sweet Mustard Dressing.

Sweet Mustard Dressing

1/4 cup whole grain mustard
1/4 cup lemon juice
2 tablespoons water
2 tablespoons red wine vinegar
1 tablespoon honey
1 tablespoon chopped fresh parsley
Kosher salt to taste
Freshly ground pepper to taste
1 cup peanut oil
Water

Makes 2 cups

Combine the mustard, lemon juice, water, vinegar, honey, parsley, salt and pepper in a bowl and mix well. Add the peanut oil slowly, whisking constantly until blended. You may add additional water to reach the desired consistency if the dressing is too thick. Store the dressing in a jar with a tight-fitting lid in the refrigerator for up to 3 weeks.

Caesar Salad

4 cups torn romaine
20 to 24 seasoned croutons
Creamy Caesar Dressing (below)
2 tablespoons shredded
    Parmesan cheese

Serves 2

Combine the lettuce, croutons and the desired amount of Creamy Caesar Dressing in a bowl and toss to coat. Divide equally between two salad plates. Sprinkle with the Parmesan cheese.

Creamy Caesar Dressing

$1/2$ cup (2 ounces) grated
    Parmesan cheese
1 cup mayonnaise
1 tablespoon milk
1 tablespoon lemon juice
1 teaspoon Dijon mustard
$1/2$ teaspoon Worcestershire sauce
$1/4$ teaspoon kosher salt
$1/4$ teaspoon freshly ground pepper
1 garlic clove, minced
1 anchovy fillet, minced
Water

Makes 2 cups

Combine the cheese, mayonnaise, milk, lemon juice, Dijon mustard, Worcestershire sauce, salt, pepper, garlic and anchovy in a bowl and whisk until blended. You may add water to reach the desired consistency if the dressing is too thick. Store the dressing in a jar with a tight-fitting lid in the refrigerator for up to 10 days.

53

Mediterranean Salad

4 cups mixed salad greens
10 kalamata olives
4 marinated artichoke hearts,
    cut into halves
1/2 cup sliced roasted red pepper
Parmesan Italian Dressing (below)

Serves 2

Toss the salad greens, olives, artichoke hearts, red pepper and the desired amount of Parmesan Italian Dressing together in a bowl. Divide equally between two chilled salad plates.

Parmesan Italian Dressing

1/2 cup water
2 tablespoons lemon juice
2 tablespoons red wine vinegar
1 teaspoon sugar
1/2 teaspoon dried oregano
1/2 teaspoon dried basil
1/4 teaspoon garlic powder
1 tablespoon finely chopped
    white onion
1/4 cup (1 ounce) grated
    Parmesan cheese
1 cup peanut oil

Makes 2 cups

Combine the water, lemon juice, vinegar, sugar, oregano, basil, garlic powder, onion and cheese in a bowl and mix well. Add the peanut oil slowly, whisking constantly until blended. Store the dressing in a jar with a tight-fitting lid in the refrigerator for up to 3 weeks.

California Salad

4 cups mixed salad greens
2 tablespoons chopped walnuts
6 slices Roma tomato
2 tablespoons crumbled
    Gorgonzola cheese
Raspberry Walnut Vinaigrette
    (page 47)

Serves 2

Toss the salad greens and walnuts together in a bowl. Divide equally between two salad plates. Top with the tomato slices. Sprinkle with the cheese and drizzle with the desired amount of Raspberry Walnut Vinaigrette.

The Melting Pot in the News

"Fondue fans can have a feast at The Melting Pot at the new Thousand Oaks restaurant…It is one of the most attractive eating spaces around, with gleaming dark wood and niches for groups who want to share the novel experience…Best of all was the first course. The cheeses swirled into a perfect consistency for dipping, and the flavor seemed just right…We were particularly pleased with the salads, each fresh and well-seasoned… Dining at The Melting Pot is a convivial experience, one with enough options to keep you dipping for a long time."

—*Simi Valley Star*
Ventura, California
February 17, 2005

Spinach Mushroom Salad

4 cups baby spinach leaves
2 cups thinly sliced baby portobello
   mushrooms
¼ cup chopped cooked bacon
½ cup thinly sliced red onion
½ cup diced tomato
Parmesan Italian Dressing
   (page 54)

Serves 2

Mound equal amounts of the spinach on two salad plates. Sprinkle with the mushrooms and bacon. Arrange the onion over the top. Sprinkle the tomato around the edge of the salad. Drizzle with the desired amount of Parmesan Italian Dressing.

The Melting Pot in the News

"The Melting Pot of Tulsa is celebrating its second anniversary with a benefit for St. Jude Children's Research Hospital on June 25. The restaurant will offer a four-course fondue meal and a complimentary gift for a cost of $45 per person, with a portion of the proceeds going to St. Jude. As part of the celebration, guests can enter a drawing to win the grand prize of 'fondue for a year'—one fondue dinner for two per month for 12 consecutive months."

—*Tulsa World*
Tulsa, Oklahoma
January 23, 2007

Antipasti

2 cups mixed salad greens
8 ounces salami, thinly sliced
8 ounces prosciutto, thinly sliced
8 ounces mortadella, sliced
4 ounces fresh Mozzarella
  cheese, sliced
4 ounces Provolone cheese, cubed
7 anchovy fillets
1/4 cup green olives
1/4 cup kalamata olives
7 grape tomatoes, cut into halves
3/4 cup marinated artichoke
  heart halves
1/4 cup aged balsamic vinegar
1/2 cup extra-virgin olive oil

Serves 6 to 8

Arrange the salad greens evenly over a large platter. Arrange the salami, prosciutto, mortadella, Mozzarella cheese, Provolone cheese, anchovies, green olives, kalamata olives, tomatoes and artichoke hearts over the salad greens. Drizzle with the vinegar and olive oil. Serve with Italian bread.

Athenian Salad

4 cups iceberg lettuce and romaine mix
1/4 cup sliced pepperoni
2 tablespoons diced ham
2 tablespoons crumbled Feta cheese
2 tablespoons garbanzo beans
White Balsamic Vinaigrette (page 50)
2 tablespoons grated Parmesan cheese
2 tablespoons sliced roasted red pepper
10 kalamata olives

Serves 2

Combine the lettuce mix, pepperoni, ham, Feta cheese, garbanzo beans and the desired amount of White Balsamic Vinaigrette in a bowl and toss gently. Divide the mixture evenly between two salad bowls. Sprinkle with the Parmesan cheese. Arrange the red pepper in the center of each salad. Arrange the olives around the red pepper.

When you walk into any of The Melting Pot locations across the country, one of the first things you are bound to notice is the delicious aroma that permeates the air. While The Melting Pot has gained notoriety thanks to its cheese and chocolate fondues, that signature Melting Pot aroma comes from the entrée cooking styles. Our chefs have pulled together the best of hot pot cooking from around the globe, then tweaked and tested each method until they perfected the favorites you'll find on our menu today.

Entrée fondue cooking styles run the gamut of textures, flavors, and aromas. The pop and sizzle of the traditional oil-cooked Bourguignonne Cooking Style makes use of flavorful batters to give meat and vegetables crisp layers of taste, while the lighter vegetable broth fondue offers a health-conscious alternative in a style that's equally traditional.

Hot Pots of the World

The bold citrus zest of the Cuban-inspired Mojo Cooking Style adds spice to seafood and chicken, and the rich flavors of the red wine-based Coq au Vin Cooking Style is a long-standing favorite. You can customize each style to suit your taste by using different oils, broths, herbs, or wines. And just like our restaurants, your kitchen will have that delicious aroma that tells you something that's perfectly suited to your taste is cooking.

For those in search of more flavors, marinades and rubs infuse the meats and vegetables with bursts of intense taste. A good marinade can tenderize meat and lock in the natural juices, while a great rub can add ethnic twists like Cajun or Asian flavors.

We share some of our favorite rubs, marinades, and cooking styles here to help you re-create the moment in your home.

Panang Curry Chicken Marinade

¹/₂ cup packed light brown sugar

¹/₄ cup red curry paste

1 (14-ounce) can unsweetened
 coconut milk

1 tablespoon lemon juice

1 teaspoon ginger

1 tablespoon paprika

2 pounds chicken, cubed

Serves 8 to 10

Combine the brown sugar, curry paste, coconut milk, lemon juice, ginger and paprika in a bowl and whisk until blended. Add the chicken and toss by hand until coated. Marinate, covered, in the refrigerator for 8 hours or longer or for 24 hours or longer if using whole pieces of chicken.

More About St. Jude

St. Jude Children's Research Hospital is a completely unique facility. Discoveries made at St. Jude have revolutionized the treatment of pediatric cancer and other catastrophic diseases. Doctors across the world send their toughest cases and most vulnerable patients to St. Jude, and it is America's third largest health-care charity. But what really makes St. Jude special is that all patients are accepted and treated without regard to the family's ability to pay. For more information, please visit www.stjude.org.

Caribbean Jerk Rub

1 tablespoon Old Bay seasoning
1 tablespoon ground coriander
1 tablespoon brown sugar
1 1/2 teaspoons onion powder
1 1/2 teaspoons garlic powder
1 1/2 teaspoons cayenne pepper
1 1/2 teaspoons kosher salt
1 teaspoon freshly ground
    black pepper
1 teaspoon dried thyme
1/2 teaspoon cinnamon
1/2 teaspoon allspice
1/2 teaspoon ground cloves
1 pound beef or chicken, cubed

Serves 4 to 6

Combine the Old Bay seasoning, coriander, brown sugar, onion powder, garlic powder, cayenne pepper, salt, black pepper, thyme, cinnamon, allspice and cloves in a bowl and mix well. Add the beef and toss by hand until coated. Marinate, covered, in the refrigerator for 30 minutes or longer or for 2 hours or longer if using larger pieces of meat. You may also use this rub for your favorite seafood.

Dipping Etiquette for Entrées

When eating fondue as an entrée, a piece of meat or a vegetable should be speared firmly while on its own plate with the fondue fork and carefully placed into the pot of hot oil or broth. The food should be allowed to sit until cooked to your taste and then removed from the pot. Using your dinner fork, slide the food off of the fondue fork and onto your plate. Also use your dinner fork for dipping the cooked food into sauces or seasonings and for eating.

Jamaican Pepper Marinade

2 tablespoons garlic chili paste
2 tablespoons olive oil
Zest of 1/2 lime
Juice of 1/2 lime
1 teaspoon freshly ground pepper
1/2 teaspoon kosher salt
1 pound chicken, cubed

Serves 4 to 6

Whisk the chili paste, olive oil, lime zest, lime juice, pepper and salt in a bowl until combined. Add the chicken and toss by hand until coated. Marinate, covered, in the refrigerator for 30 minutes or longer or for 4 hours or longer if using larger pieces of meat. You may also use this marinade for your favorite seafood.

Greek Marinade

1/2 cup lemon juice
1/4 cup olive oil
1 tablespoon honey
1 tablespoon dried oregano
Kosher salt to taste
Freshly ground pepper to taste
8 ounces beef or chicken, cubed

Serves 2 to 4

Whisk the lemon juice, olive oil, honey, oregano, salt and pepper in a bowl until combined. Add the beef and toss by hand until coated. Marinate, covered, in the refrigerator for 30 minutes or longer or for 4 hours or longer if using larger pieces of meat. You may also use this marinade for your favorite seafood.

Chimichurri Marinade

1 bunch parsley, coarsely chopped
8 garlic cloves, finely chopped
1 tablespoon finely chopped
   red onion
3/4 cup extra-virgin olive oil
1/4 cup red wine vinegar
Juice of 1/2 lemon
1 teaspoon dried oregano
1 teaspoon freshly ground pepper
1/2 teaspoon kosher salt
1 pound beef or chicken, cubed

Serves 4 to 6

Whisk the parsley, garlic, onion, olive oil, vinegar, lemon juice, oregano, pepper and salt in a bowl until combined. Add the beef and toss by hand until coated. Marinate, covered, in the refrigerator for 30 minutes or longer or for 4 hours or longer if using larger pieces of meat.

Fondue Myths and Legends

There are some funny myths that have sprung up around fondue and its power to bring people together. One such legend is that fondue was used as part of a sixteenth-century Swiss peace treaty between feuding religions during the Reformation. According to the story, the Protestants brought the bread, the Catholics brought the wine, and the Anabaptists brought the cheese. Then everyone sat down and ate fondue together as a way to kick off the negotiations!

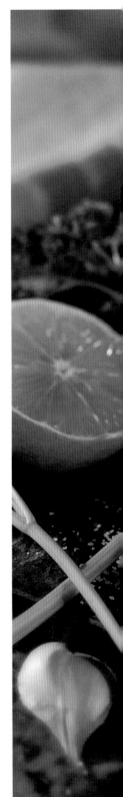

Antipasti

2 cups mixed salad greens
8 ounces salami, thinly sliced
8 ounces prosciutto, thinly sliced
8 ounces mortadella, sliced
4 ounces fresh Mozzarella
   cheese, sliced
4 ounces Provolone cheese, cubed
7 anchovy fillets
1/4 cup green olives
1/4 cup kalamata olives
7 grape tomatoes, cut into halves
3/4 cup marinated artichoke
   heart halves
1/4 cup aged balsamic vinegar
1/2 cup extra-virgin olive oil

Serves 6 to 8

Arrange the salad greens evenly over a large platter. Arrange the salami, prosciutto, mortadella, Mozzarella cheese, Provolone cheese, anchovies, green olives, kalamata olives, tomatoes and artichoke hearts over the salad greens. Drizzle with the vinegar and olive oil. Serve with Italian bread.

Athenian Salad

4 cups iceberg lettuce and romaine mix
1/4 cup sliced pepperoni
2 tablespoons diced ham
2 tablespoons crumbled Feta cheese
2 tablespoons garbanzo beans
White Balsamic Vinaigrette (page 50)
2 tablespoons grated Parmesan cheese
2 tablespoons sliced roasted red pepper
10 kalamata olives

Serves 2

Combine the lettuce mix, pepperoni, ham, Feta cheese, garbanzo beans and the desired amount of White Balsamic Vinaigrette in a bowl and toss gently. Divide the mixture evenly between two salad bowls. Sprinkle with the Parmesan cheese. Arrange the red pepper in the center of each salad. Arrange the olives around the red pepper.

Sesame Soy Marinade

2 tablespoons warm water

2 tablespoons light brown sugar

1/4 cup soy sauce

1 tablespoon sesame oil

2 tablespoons finely chopped
  scallions

1 teaspoon finely chopped garlic

1/2 teaspoon ginger

1/4 teaspoon freshly ground pepper

1 pound beef or chicken, cubed

Serves 4 to 6

Combine the water and brown sugar in a bowl and whisk until the brown sugar is dissolved. Add the soy sauce, sesame oil, scallions, garlic, ginger and pepper and whisk until combined. Add the beef and toss by hand until coated. Marinate, covered, in the refrigerator for 3 hours or longer or for 8 hours or longer if using larger pieces of meat.

Teriyaki Marinade

3/4 cup soy sauce

1/4 cup packed light brown sugar

1/4 cup water

1/4 cup rice wine vinegar

1 tablespoon sesame oil

3 garlic cloves, finely chopped

1 (1-inch) piece fresh ginger, peeled
  and finely chopped

1 pound beef or chicken, cubed

Serves 4 to 6

Combine the soy sauce, brown sugar, water, vinegar, sesame oil, garlic and ginger in a small saucepan and bring to a boil, whisking constantly. Place in the refrigerator until completely cool. Combine with the beef in a bowl and toss by hand until the beef is coated. Marinate, covered, in the refrigerator for 2 hours or longer or for 4 hours or longer if using larger pieces of meat.

Mustard and Rosemary Marinade

1/4 cup lemon juice
1/4 cup olive oil
3 tablespoons whole grain mustard
1 garlic clove, finely chopped
1 tablespoon finely chopped
   fresh rosemary
1 teaspoon kosher salt
1 pound chicken, cubed

Serves 4 to 6

Whisk the lemon juice, olive oil, mustard, garlic, rosemary and salt in a bowl until combined. Add the chicken and toss by hand until coated. Marinate, covered, in the refrigerator for 30 minutes or longer. You may also use this marinade for your favorite seafood.

What Our Guests Say

"My wife made reservations at The Melting Pot for a late Valentine's Day dinner. I'm always out of town, and we don't get to spend much time together. When our entrée came, our server overheard me complaining, but she told me to shut my eyes. She explained that fondue was about the experience. When I opened my eyes, she had all of our food cooking. She said, 'I don't want our concept to get in the way of the reason you came here.' In that moment, I looked at my wife and told her how much I loved her. She had tears in her eyes and she said, 'I know we always say it, but that's the first time in a while that I've felt you really meant it.' The rest of the evening was peaceful and romantic. I will never forget that young girl who helped us fall in love again."

—G. Welch
Oklahoma City, Oklahoma

71

Cilantro-Lime Marinade

Juice of 2 limes
1/2 cup olive oil
1 garlic clove, finely chopped
2 tablespoons chopped
    fresh cilantro
2 teaspoons sugar
1/2 teaspoon chili powder
1/2 teaspoon cumin
1/2 teaspoon red pepper flakes
Kosher salt to taste
Freshly ground black pepper
    to taste
1 pound chicken, cubed

Serves 4 to 6

Whisk the lime juice, olive oil, garlic, cilantro, sugar, chili powder, cumin, red pepper flakes, salt and black pepper in a bowl until combined. Add the chicken and toss by hand until coated. Marinate, covered, in the refrigerator for 30 minutes or longer or for 4 hours or longer if using larger pieces of meat. You may also use this marinade for your favorite seafood.

Fondue Party Tips

Throwing a fondue party is an easy and fun way to bring friends and family together. Here are a few tips to make sure everything goes smoothly—and safely!

Have a separate fondue fork for each guest. Mark each fondue fork with a different color or charm so that guests can tell them apart.

Cut all the food to be dipped into bite-size pieces.

Make sure that guests have separate plates for their raw meat and their cooked food.

Never leave fondue pots unattended.

Balsamic Marinade

1 cup balsamic vinegar
1 tablespoon light brown sugar
1 tablespoon soy sauce
1 1/2 teaspoons honey
1 pound beef, cubed

Serves 4 to 6

Cook the vinegar in a saucepan over medium heat for 10 to 12 minutes or until reduced by three-fourths. Whisk in the brown sugar, soy sauce and honey. Pour into a bowl and chill, uncovered, for 30 to 45 minutes. Add the beef and toss by hand until coated. Marinate, covered, in the refrigerator for 8 hours or longer or for 24 hours or longer if using larger pieces of meat.

Garlic and Herb Marinade

8 garlic cloves
2 tablespoons vegetable oil
1 tablespoon chopped
   fresh parsley
1 teaspoon dried basil
1 1/2 teaspoons kosher salt
1 pound chicken, cubed

Serves 4 to 6

Sauté the garlic in the oil in a sauté pan for 15 minutes. Strain, reserving the oil. Let the garlic cool. Chop the garlic. Combine the garlic with the reserved oil, parsley, basil and salt in a bowl and mix well. Add the chicken and toss by hand until coated. Marinate, covered, in the refrigerator for 30 minutes or longer or for 4 hours or longer if using larger pieces of meat. You may also use this marinade for your favorite seafood.

Mojo Cooking Style

5¹/₂ cups warm water
Juice of ¹/₂ orange
Juice of ¹/₂ lime
3 tablespoons finely chopped onion
1 tablespoon finely chopped celery
1 tablespoon finely chopped carrot
1 tablespoon finely chopped garlic
2 tablespoons chopped fresh
    cilantro
2 tablespoons kosher salt
1 tablespoon freshly ground pepper

Whisk the water, orange juice, lime juice, onion, celery, carrot, garlic, cilantro, salt and pepper in a bowl until combined. Pour into a fondue pot. Bring to a rapid simmer over medium-high heat. Thread a piece of meat or vegetable on a fondue fork. Cook in the broth to the desired degree of doneness. Serve with your favorite sauce.

Finding the Perfect Fondue Pot—Entrée Fondues

A pot made of stainless steel is the ideal choice for preparing entrée fondues. However, many metal pots come with a ceramic insert for preparing cheese and chocolate fondues without buying a separate pot. There are two types of metal fondue pots: electric or the old-fashioned open-flame variety. Electric pots are wonderful because they allow you to easily control temperature, but today's open-flame pots have new types of fuels, such as gels, that are easy to use as well.

Voodoo Cooking Style

5¹/₂ cups warm water
Juice of ¹/₂ orange
Juice of ¹/₄ lime
3 tablespoons finely chopped onion
1 tablespoon finely chopped celery
1 tablespoon finely chopped carrot
1 tablespoon finely chopped garlic
2 tablespoons chopped fresh
   cilantro
2 tablespoons kosher salt
1 tablespoon freshly ground pepper
3 tablespoons blackened seasoning
   (Paul Prudhomme's Blackened
   Redfish Magic recommended)

Whisk the water, orange juice, lime juice, onion, celery, carrot, garlic, cilantro, salt, pepper and blackened seasoning in a bowl until combined. Pour into a fondue pot. Bring to a rapid simmer over medium-high heat. Thread a piece of meat or vegetable on a fondue fork. Cook in the broth to the desired degree of doneness. Serve with your favorite sauce.

Finding the Perfect Fondue Pot—Fondue Forks

There are quite a few options when it comes to choosing fondue forks to go with your new fondue pot, but we have a few tips to make sure you chose the right forks for you! Look for fondue forks with color-coordinated handles. The colors help guests keep track of their food while it's cooking. Forks with barbs on the end help keep food from falling off and into the pot, and thick metal forks are less likely to bend when cleaned.

Court Bouillon Cooking Style

5 1/2 cups warm water
3 tablespoons finely chopped onion
1 tablespoon finely chopped celery
1 tablespoon finely chopped carrot
2 tablespoons kosher salt
1 tablespoon freshly ground pepper
2 teaspoons garlic powder

Whisk the water, onion, celery, carrot, salt, pepper and garlic powder in a bowl until combined. Pour into a fondue pot. Bring to a rapid simmer over medium-high heat. Thread a piece of meat or vegetable on a fondue fork. Cook in the broth to the desired degree of doneness. Serve with your favorite sauce.

Garlic and Wine Seasoning

Two culinary classics—garlic and wine—give our signature seasoning its unique flavor. The Melting Pot's Garlic and Wine Seasoning is extremely versatile. It's great sprinkled on salads, mixed with olive oil as a dipping sauce for breads, used as a rub for grilling meats and vegetables, or mixed with olive oil, lemon juice, and minced onion for the perfect marinade. And, of course, it's the perfect complement to cheese and entrée fondues!

Luau Cooking Style

4 cups low-sodium chicken broth
1 cup pineapple juice
1/2 cup soy sauce
1/2 teaspoon ginger
3 garlic cloves, thinly sliced

Whisk the broth, pineapple juice, soy sauce, ginger and garlic in a bowl until combined. Pour into a fondue pot. Bring to a rapid simmer over medium-high heat. Thread a piece of meat or vegetable on a fondue fork. Cook in the broth to the desired degree of doneness. Serve with your favorite sauce.

Celebrations at The Melting Pot

The Melting Pot is a great place to celebrate! Nothing brings friends and family together like a delicious, communal meal, and at The Melting Pot we are always happy to make sure your celebration with us is a special one. For large celebrations, we can work with you ahead of time to prepare set menus and decorate a private space for you and your guests. For smaller celebrations, we can have decorations or a special bottle of wine waiting for you and your guests.

Coq au Vin Cooking Style

3³/4 cups warm water

1¹/2 cups burgundy

³/4 cup thinly sliced button
   mushrooms

¹/4 cup chopped scallions

3 tablespoons finely chopped onion

2 tablespoons finely chopped garlic

1 tablespoon finely chopped celery

1 tablespoon finely chopped carrot

2 tablespoons kosher salt

1 tablespoon freshly ground pepper

Whisk the water, wine, mushrooms, scallions, onion, garlic, celery, carrot, salt and pepper in a bowl until combined. Pour into a fondue pot. Bring to a rapid simmer over medium-high heat. Thread a piece of meat or vegetable on a fondue fork. Cook in the broth to the desired degree of doneness. Serve with your favorite sauce.

Gourmet Ingredients

Each fondue is only as good as the ingredients that go into it. Higher quality ingredients such as gourmet cheeses and chocolates, extra-virgin olive oil, fresh herbs and vegetables, and choice cuts of meat will make a world of difference in the flavors of your fondues. Gourmet ingredients can be a little pricey, so if you are cooking on a tight budget you can mix a more expensive version of your cheese or chocolate with a less expensive version to get more flavor without breaking the bank.

Zen Cooking Style

5 1/2 cups warm water
Juice of 1/2 lime
3 tablespoons chopped lemongrass
3 tablespoons finely chopped onion
1 tablespoon finely chopped celery
1 tablespoon finely chopped carrot
2 tablespoons kosher salt
1 tablespoon freshly ground pepper
1 tablespoon ginger
2 teaspoons garlic powder

Whisk the water, lime juice, lemongrass, onion, celery, carrot, salt, pepper, ginger and garlic powder in a bowl until combined. Pour into a fondue pot. Bring to a rapid simmer over medium-high heat. Thread a piece of meat or vegetable on a fondue fork. Cook in the broth to the desired degree of doneness. Serve with your favorite sauce.

Finding the Perfect Fondue Pot—All the Extras

Once you've found the perfect fondue set for you, it's time to stock up on the extras that make fondueing safe and easy. Raclette plates help your guests keep different sauces and meats separate while they are dining, and it's always good to have several small sauce containers on hand so that the sauces can be passed around easily. And don't forget to keep extra fuel on hand for nonelectric pots—you wouldn't want to run out halfway through a meal!

Bourguignonne Cooking Style

3 to 5 cups (24 to 40 ounces)
vegetable oil or peanut oil

Fill a fondue pot one-third full with oil. Heat the oil to 350 degrees, following any safety warnings that your fondue set may include regarding the heating of oil. Thread a piece of meat on a fondue fork. Cook the meat in the hot oil to the desired degree of doneness. Let the remaining oil cool and discard safely.

Note—To prevent splattering during the cooking process, make certain that the meat is at room temperature and has been blotted dry to eliminate excess moisture.

Fondue Cooking Tip— Cooking with Oils

There are many delicious oil choices available for the Bourguignonne Cooking Style. At The Melting Pot, we use pure canola oil for its mild taste. However, you can use different oils to achieve different flavors in your cooked foods. Peanut oil adds a slightly sweet flavor to meats and vegetables, while olive oil adds a rich, warm taste. Vegetable oil is always a popular choice, and grapeseed oil is becoming a favored fondue oil thanks to its nutty flavor.

Sesame Batter

1 egg yolk
1 cup all-purpose flour
1 cup ice cold tonic water
1/4 cup cornstarch
1 tablespoon black sesame seeds
1 tablespoon white sesame seeds
1 teaspoon kosher salt
1 teaspoon freshly ground pepper
2 tablespoons sesame oil
Assorted chopped vegetables

Makes 2¹/2 cups batter

Purée the egg yolk, flour, water, cornstarch, black sesame seeds, white sesame seeds, salt, pepper and sesame oil in a blender until smooth. Pour into a shallow bowl. Thread vegetables on a fondue forks and dip into the batter, turning to coat evenly. Submerge carefully in hot oil in a fondue pot and cook to the desired degree of doneness. Discard any remaining batter.

Note—Use the batter immediately or chill for no more than 2 hours before using. Use only with the Bourguignonne Cooking Style.

Tempura Batter

1 egg yolk
1 cup all-purpose flour
1 cup ice cold tonic water
1/4 cup cornstarch
1 tablespoon paprika
1 teaspoon kosher salt
1 teaspoon freshly ground pepper
Assorted chopped vegetables

Makes 2¹/2 cups batter

Purée the egg yolk, flour, water, cornstarch, paprika, salt and pepper in a blender until smooth. Pour into a shallow bowl. Thread vegetables on fondue forks and dip into the batter, turning to coat evenly. Submerge carefully in hot oil in a fondue pot and cook to the desired degree of doneness. Discard any remaining batter.

Note—Use the batter immediately or chill for no more than 2 hours before using. Use only with the Bourguignonne Cooking Style.

A pretty woman is more beautiful in a gorgeous dress, and a good entrée is transformed into a great entrée by a delicious sauce.

An array of sauces with a fondue meal is a wonderful touch. In fact, most would agree that it completes the experience. The zip of teriyaki, the kick of horseradish, the sweet spice of a Thai peanut sauce — each one lends its distinctive goodness to a morsel of meat or cut of vegetable.

We have selected some of our favorites and a few new selections straight from our Research and Development Kitchen that will allow you to Dip into Something Different!®

A Touch of Extra Taste

Spicy Thai Peanut Sauce

1/2 cup orange juice
1/4 cup Chinese plum sauce
1/4 cup crunchy peanut butter
1 tablespoon finely chopped red
    bell pepper
1 tablespoon finely chopped green
    bell pepper
1 tablespoon soy sauce
1 tablespoon balsamic vinegar
1 tablespoon lemon juice
1 tablespoon dry mustard
1 tablespoon ginger
1 teaspoon sugar
1/2 teaspoon kosher salt
1/2 cup peanut oil
2 teaspoons sesame oil

Makes 2 1/2 cups

Combine the orange juice, plum sauce, peanut butter, bell peppers, soy sauce, vinegar, lemon juice, mustard, ginger, sugar and salt in a food processor and process until smooth. Add the peanut oil and sesame oil gradually, processing constantly until blended.

History of St. Jude
St. Jude's began as the answer to a prayer. Danny Thomas, then a struggling young entertainer, knelt before a statue of St. Jude Thaddeus, the patron saint of hopeless causes, and prayed for the saint to show him his way in life. Thomas's career prospered through films and television, and he became a nationally known entertainer. Eager to give back to the saint that had so inspired him in his youth, Thomas dreamed of founding a children's research center in Memphis, Tennessee.

Thomas raised money throughout the 1950s and in 1962, St. Jude Children's Research Hospital opened its doors. It is now one of the world's premier centers for the study and treatment of catastrophic diseases in children. Through improvements in the care of pediatric leukemia and numerous forms of solid tumors, Danny Thomas's "little hospital in Memphis" has brought about improved health care for children all over the world.

Ginger Soy Sauce

1 cup soy sauce
2 tablespoons chili sauce
2 tablespoons light brown sugar
$1/2$ teaspoon ginger
1 cup fresh orange juice

Makes 2 cups

Combine the soy sauce, chili sauce, brown sugar and ginger in a bowl and whisk until blended. Scrape the side of the bowl with a rubber spatula. Whisk in the orange juice. Chill, covered, until serving time.

Ginger Soy Wasabi Sauce

1 cup low-sodium soy sauce
$1/4$ cup honey
1 tablespoon chopped fresh ginger
2 tablespoons wasabi paste

Makes $1^1/2$ cups

Combine the soy sauce, honey, ginger and wasabi paste in a bowl and whisk until blended.

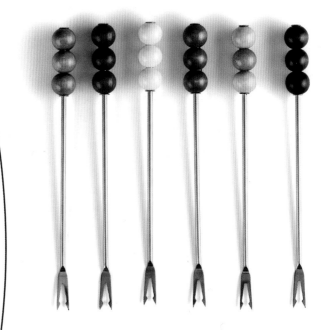

Hoisin Dipping Sauce

1/2 cup hoisin sauce
1/4 cup fresh lime juice
2 tablespoons orange juice
1 tablespoon chopped scallions
Salt and pepper to taste

Makes 3/4 cup

Whisk the hoisin sauce, lime juice, orange juice and scallions in a bowl until combined. Season with salt and pepper.

Hot Honey Citrus Sauce

2 tablespoons wasabi powder
1/2 cup orange juice
1 cup orange marmalade
1/2 cup honey
2 tablespoons Dijon mustard

Makes 2 cups

Dissolve the wasabi powder in the orange juice in a bowl using a wire whisk. Add the marmalade, honey and Dijon mustard and whisk until blended.

Island Sauce

¹/₂ cup orange marmalade
Juice of ¹/₂ lime
1 garlic clove, minced
1 teaspoon chopped fresh parsley
1 teaspoon kosher salt
¹/₂ teaspoon cayenne pepper
¹/₂ teaspoon onion powder
¹/₄ teaspoon freshly ground
   black pepper

Makes ³/₄ cup

Combine the marmalade, lime juice, garlic, parsley, salt, cayenne pepper, onion powder and black pepper in a bowl and whisk until combined.

Fun Fondue Fork-lore— The Caquelon

Traditionally, fondue was prepared in a caquelon—a pot made of heavy earthenware, glazed ceramic, or enameled iron to help distribute heat evenly and retain heat for longer periods of time. Originally, peasants more commonly used the earthenware varieties because they were more affordable, while the upper classes favored iron pots. Today, fondue pots of all types are affordable, so pick whichever you prefer!

Mild Lemon Chili Sauce

1 cup chili sauce
1 1/2 tablespoons fresh lemon juice
Zest of 1 lemon, grated

Makes 1 cup

Combine the chili sauce, lemon juice and lemon zest in a blender and process until blended. Serve at room temperature.

Spicy Cocktail Sauce

1 cup ketchup
2 tablespoons apple cider vinegar
1/4 teaspoon Worcestershire sauce
2 tablespoons prepared
    horseradish
Juice of 1 lemon
Hot red pepper sauce to taste

Makes 1 1/2 cups

Combine the ketchup, vinegar, Worcestershire sauce, horseradish, lemon juice and hot sauce in a bowl and whisk until blended. Chill, covered, until serving time.

Tartar Sauce

3/4 cup mayonnaise
2 tablespoons chopped green onions
    or scallions
2 tablespoons drained sweet
    pickle relish
1 tablespoon chopped
    drained capers
1 tablespoon chopped fresh parsley
1 teaspoon finely chopped fresh
    tarragon
1 teaspoon fresh lemon juice

Makes 1 cup

Whisk the mayonnaise, green onions, pickle relish, capers, parsley, tarragon and lemon juice in a bowl until combined. May be served at room temperature or chilled.

Garden Herb Aïoli Sauce

1 1/2 cups mayonnaise
1/4 cup chopped fresh parsley
1 1/2 teaspoons chopped fresh chives
1 teaspoon chopped fresh dill weed
1 teaspoon chopped fresh tarragon
1 teaspoon Dijon mustard
Salt and pepper to taste

Makes 2 cups

Combine the mayonnaise, parsley, chives, dill weed and tarragon in a bowl and mix well. Stir in the Dijon mustard. Season with salt and pepper. Chill, covered, until serving time.

Creamy Curry Dipping Sauce

1/2 cup plain yogurt

1/2 cup mayonnaise

1/2 cup mango chutney
   (Major Grey's recommended)

2 teaspoons minced red onion

2 teaspoons curry powder

1 teaspoon fresh lime juice

1/4 teaspoon cayenne pepper

Makes 2 cups

Combine the yogurt, mayonnaise, chutney, onion, curry powder, lime juice and cayenne pepper in a food processor and pulse two or three times or until the desired consistency is reached. Spoon into a bowl. Chill, covered, for 2 hours or longer before serving. May be stored, covered, in the refrigerator for up to 3 days.

The Melting Pot in the News

"The owners of The Melting Pot say they're pretty confident about the reception they're getting locally for their new upscale, casual restaurant. The Tampa-based franchise opens its 5,500-square foot restaurant today at the Avenue Viera retail center. Bernard Letzinger, co-owner of the franchise restaurant, said all seats are booked through Sunday. 'It's all word-of-mouth,' said Letzinger, a University of Florida graduate who lives in Satellite Beach. 'We urge people to call and make reservtions.'"

—*Florida Today*
Melbourne, Florida
March 16, 2005

Creamy Cucumber Sauce

1 cucumber, peeled and grated
1/2 teaspoon kosher salt
1/2 cup sour cream
1/2 cup mayonnaise
1 tablespoon minced onion
1/2 teaspoon Worcestershire sauce

Makes 1 1/2 cups

Place the cucumber in a cheesecloth or kitchen towel and sprinkle with the salt. Wrap the cheesecloth around the cucumber and place in a colander set in the sink. Place weights, such as soup cans on the wrapped cucumber. Let stand until well drained. Unwrap the cucumber and combine with the sour cream, mayonnaise, onion and Worcestershire sauce in a bowl and mix well.

Horseradish Cream Sauce

1 cup sour cream
3 tablespoons prepared
   horseradish
2 teaspoons fresh lemon juice
1/4 teaspoon Worcestershire sauce
2 scallions, finely chopped
Salt and pepper to taste

Makes 1 1/2 cups

Whisk the sour cream, horseradish, lemon juice, Worcestershire sauce, scallions, salt and pepper in a bowl until combined.

New Orleans–Style Remoulade Sauce

1 cup mayonnaise
1/2 cup prepared horseradish
1/4 cup fresh lemon juice
1/4 cup Creole mustard or
  Dijon mustard
2 tablespoons Worcestershire sauce
1 tablespoon sweet pickle relish
1 tablespoon capers
1 teaspoon apple cider vinegar
Juice of 1 lime
1 shallot, finely chopped
1 garlic clove, finely chopped
1/4 cup chopped celery
1/4 cup chopped scallions
3 tablespoons paprika
1 tablespoon blackened seasoning
2 teaspoons chopped fresh parsley
1 1/2 teaspoons kosher salt
1 teaspoon ground cloves
1/2 teaspoon dried thyme
Freshly ground pepper to taste

Makes 3 cups

Combine the mayonnaise, horseradish, lemon juice, Creole mustard, Worcestershire sauce, pickle relish, capers, vinegar, lime juice, shallot, garlic, celery, scallions, paprika, blackened seasoning, parsley, salt, cloves, thyme and pepper in a food processor and process for 30 seconds. Spoon into a bowl and chill, covered, until serving time.

 Fondue Cooking Tip
Garlic is a key ingredient in many of The Melting Pot's recipes. But how do you get the smell of garlic off of your fingers once you've peeled and chopped it for use in your cheese fondue and sauces? Rub your fingers on a stainless steel teaspoon before washing them, and the odor will be gone!

Roasted Red Pepper Sauce

1 cup sour cream
1/4 cup mayonnaise
2 tablespoons lemon juice
1/2 (28-ounce) can roasted red
    peppers, drained and rinsed
1 tablespoon Dijon mustard
1 tablespoon prepared horseradish
1 teaspoon chopped garlic
1/2 teaspoon cayenne pepper
1/2 teaspoon kosher salt
1/2 teaspoon freshly ground
    black pepper

Makes 2 cups

Combine the sour cream, mayonnaise, lemon juice, red peppers, Dijon mustard, horseradish, garlic, cayenne pepper, salt and black pepper in a food processor and process until smooth. Spoon into a bowl and chill, covered, for 30 minutes or longer before serving.

Red Mustard Sauce

3/4 cup ketchup
1/4 cup water
1 tablespoon whole grain mustard
1 tablespoon fresh lemon juice
1 1/2 teaspoons dry mustard
1 teaspoon kosher salt

Makes 1 1/2 cups

Combine the ketchup, water, whole grain mustard, lemon juice, dry mustard and salt in a food processor or blender and process until blended. Spoon into a bowl and chill, covered, until serving time.

100

Herb Butter Dipping Sauce

1 cup (2 sticks) butter, softened
2 tablespoons lemon juice
1 tablespoon chopped fresh chives
1 tablespoon chopped fresh parsley
1 tablespoon chopped fresh
   tarragon
Hot red pepper sauce to taste

Makes 1 1/2 cups

Combine the butter, lemon juice, chives, parsley, tarragon and hot sauce in a bowl and mix well. Spoon into a warm fondue pot and heat until melted.

Honey Mustard Dipping Sauce

1/2 cup mayonnaise
2 tablespoons honey
2 tablespoons Creole mustard or
   whole grain mustard
Salt to taste
Cayenne pepper to taste

Makes 3/4 cup

Combine the mayonnaise, honey, Creole mustard, salt and cayenne pepper in a bowl and whisk until blended.

Green Goddess Sauce

3/4 cup cubed softened cream cheese
1/2 cup milk
1/4 cup sour cream
1/4 cup finely chopped fresh parsley
1/4 cup finely chopped fresh chives
2 tablespoons minced white onion

Makes 2 cups

Whisk the cream cheese, milk, sour cream, parsley, chives and onion in a bowl until combined. You may also beat with an electric mixer or a hand-held mixer for 1 to 2 minutes. Chill, covered, until serving time.

Chipotle Mayonnaise

1/2 (8-ounce) can chipotle chiles in
   adobo sauce
1 cup mayonnaise
2 teaspoons Worcestershire sauce
Juice of 1 lime

Yield 1 1/2 cups

Mince the chiles and place in a bowl. Add the mayonnaise, Worcestershire sauce and lime juice and whisk until combined.

A Deep, Abiding Passion

No other food in the world has quite the same euphoria-inducing effect as chocolate. With its creamy, decadent texture, fondue really takes chocolate to the next level.

Dessert at The Melting Pot means strawberries dripping in warm milk chocolate, thick dark chocolate drizzled over fluffy cheesecake, and bananas swirled in sweet white chocolate. Whether plain or mixed with caramel, peanut butter, marshmallow creme, cookie crumbs, chopped nuts, or dessert liqueurs like amaretto and crème de menthe, chocolate fondue tends to be everyone's favorite part of a meal at The Melting Pot.

This delightful indulgence brings out something special in almost everyone. For some, feeding chocolate-dipped treats to a loved one can heighten an already romantic mood. For others, a pot of warm chocolate is the perfect conversation starter at a party. And no one enjoys the thrill of melted chocolate more than children—after all, with all of the dipping, swirling, and twirling involved, playing with your food is a fondue requirement. Whether you want the perfect ending to a romantic date, a fun party food that will put everyone in a playful mood, or just a warm and delicious dessert on a cold night—chocolate fondue will always be a welcome treat.

for Chocolate Fondue

Yin and Yang

4 ounces dark chocolate,
    finely chopped
4 ounces white chocolate,
    finely chopped

Serves 4 to 6

Melt the dark chocolate in the top of a double boiler set over simmering water, stirring constantly; or place the dark chocolate in a microwave-safe bowl and microwave until melted, stirring every 30 to 45 seconds. Be careful not to let the chocolate burn. Repeat the procedure with the white chocolate. Pour both chocolates simultaneously into a warm fondue pot. Rotate the pot one-quarter turn to produce the yin and yang effect. Garnish the white chocolate with a piece of dark chocolate and the dark chocolate with a piece of white chocolate. Keep fondue warm over low heat.

Cheese and Chocolate Fondue Dipping Etiquette

Since fondue is a communal meal, there are etiquette rules that should be followed in polite company. When eating cheese or chocolate fondue, spear a piece of food using a fondue fork, and dip it into the pot, twirling the food to coat it evenly. Make sure to eat the bite without the fondue fork touching your lips or tongue because the fork does go back into the pot. It is considered impolite to double dip the same piece of food into the pot twice.

A Deep, Abiding Passion for Chocolate Fondue

Amaretto Meltdown

8 ounces white chocolate,
  finely chopped
1 tablespoon heavy cream
2 tablespoons amaretto
1 tablespoon 151 rum

Serves 4 to 6

Combine the chocolate and cream in the top of a double boiler set over simmering water. Heat until the chocolate is melted, stirring constantly; or combine the chocolate and cream in a microwave-safe bowl and microwave until melted, stirring every 30 to 45 seconds. Be careful not to let the chocolate burn. Pour into a warm fondue pot. Add the amaretto slowly, stirring gently to combine. Pour the rum over the mixture and ignite carefully, using a long wooden match or lighter. Allow the flame to burn out and stir gently to combine. Keep fondue warm over low heat.

Chococcino

8 ounces milk chocolate,
  finely chopped
1/2 cup heavy cream
3 tablespoons espresso, or
  1 tablespoon instant
  coffee granules

Serves 4 to 6

Combine the chocolate and cream in the top of a double boiler set over simmering water. Heat until the chocolate is melted, stirring constantly; or combine the chocolate and cream in a microwave-safe bowl and microwave until melted, stirring every 30 to 45 seconds. Be careful not to let the chocolate burn. Pour into a warm fondue pot. Add the espresso and stir gently to combine. Keep fondue warm over low heat. If substituting coffee granules for the espresso, dissolve the granules in 3 tablespoons hot water before adding to the fondue pot.

Chocolate Mint Fondue

12 ounces dark chocolate,
    finely chopped
1/2 cup heavy cream
3 tablespoons crème de menthe or
    mint chocolate liqueur

Serves 4 to 6

Combine the chocolate and cream in the top of a double boiler set over simmering water. Heat until the chocolate is melted, stirring constantly; or combine the chocolate and cream in a microwave-safe bowl and microwave until melted, stirring every 30 to 45 seconds. Be careful not to let the chocolate burn. Pour into a warm fondue pot. Add the liqueur and stir gently to combine. Keep fondue warm over low heat.

Types of Chocolate—Dark

Dark chocolate is also referred to as plain chocolate since it is not mixed with any milk. Of all of the types of chocolate, dark chocolate contains the highest concentration of chocolate liquor and has a distinctly bitter taste. The strong, bitter flavor of dark chocolate fondue provides a unique contrast when paired with sweet dippers such as pineapple and marshmallows. If your chocolate fondue comes out too bitter, stir in a little confectioners' sugar until it reaches the desired level of sweetness.

Bananas Foster Fondue

4 ounces white chocolate,
    finely chopped
$1/2$ banana, thinly sliced
4 ounces caramel ice cream topping
1 teaspoon banana liqueur
1 teaspoon spiced rum

Serves 4 to 6

Melt the chocolate in the top of a double boiler set over simmering water, stirring constantly; or place the chocolate in a microwave-safe bowl and microwave until melted, stirring every 30 to 45 seconds. Be careful not to let the chocolate burn. Place the banana slices in the bottom of a warm fondue pot. Pour the chocolate over the bananas. Add the caramel and stir gently. Add the liqueur and rum and stir gently to combine. Keep fondue warm over low heat.

What Our Guests Say

"My husband and I got married and decided to have a romantic dinner that night to celebrate. Ryan was without a doubt the best waiter I've ever had. After we finished, we walked to our car only to find that he had tied balloons all over it! We were so thrilled. Some of the staff came out and applauded us as we left. This particular experience was one that I will always remember and cherish."

—Lizz Pugh

Chocolate Cream Pie Fondue

8 ounces milk chocolate,
  finely chopped
4 ounces cream cheese, cubed
1/2 cup milk
1/4 teaspoon vanilla extract

Serves 4 to 6

Melt the chocolate in the top of a double boiler set over simmering water, stirring constantly; or place the chocolate in a microwave-safe bowl and microwave until melted, stirring every 30 to 45 seconds. Be careful not to let the chocolate burn. Pour into a warm fondue pot. Add the cream cheese, milk and vanilla and stir until blended. Keep fondue warm over low heat.

Chocolate Fondue Bars
The Melting Pot's Chocolate Bars are the quickest and easiest way to make dessert fondue at home. They can be quickly melted down and mixed with flavored liqueurs, candy, or cookies to make your own chocolate fondue creations. They're even great just to nibble on, since we use only the highest quality chocolate. But what makes these bars truly sweet is that $1 of each fondue chocolate bar sold is donated to St. Jude Children's Research Hospital.

Chocolate S'mores Fondue

8 ounces milk chocolate,
  finely chopped
2 teaspoons marshmallow creme
2 tablespoons 151 rum
¹/₄ cup graham cracker crumbs

Serves 4 to 6

Melt the chocolate in the top of a double boiler set over simmering water, stirring constantly; or place the chocolate in a microwave-safe bowl and microwave until melted, stirring every 30 to 45 seconds. Be careful not to let the chocolate burn. Pour into a warm fondue pot. Spoon the marshmallow creme into the center of the chocolate. Do not stir. Add the rum to the pot and ignite carefully, using a long wooden match or lighter. Allow the flame to burn out and stir gently to combine. Sprinkle with the graham cracker crumbs. Keep fondue warm over low heat.

What Our Guests Say

Michael chose The Melting Pot, Richmond, Virginia, for his first date with Patty. Over time The Melting Pot became their special place. So when Michael decided to propose, he knew just where to go. He presented Patty with an engagement ring on the dessert plate when the chocolate fondue arrived. Patty, of course, accepted. Her only condition was that they have the wedding at The Melting Pot, Richmond, their special place, on Valentine's Day. The wedding was beautiful, and Richmond's staff was delighted to be a part of their love story. The Melting Pot, Richmond, is still Michael and Patty's special place. They even celebrated their first wedding anniversary at the same table where Michael proposed!

—The Melting Pot, Richmond, Virginia

A Deep, Abiding Passion for Chocolate Fondue

Dark Chocolate Raspberry Fondue

12 ounces dark chocolate,
  finely chopped
1/4 cup heavy cream
3 tablespoons raspberry liqueur

Serves 4 to 6

Combine the chocolate and cream in the top of a double boiler set over simmering water. Heat until the chocolate is melted, stirring constantly; or combine the chocolate and cream in a microwave-safe bowl and microwave until melted, stirring every 30 to 45 seconds. Be careful not to let the chocolate burn. Pour into a warm fondue pot. Drizzle with the liqueur. Keep fondue warm over low heat.

Love Is in the Chocolate—Romance at The Melting Pot

The Melting Pot's intimate and sophisticated atmosphere makes it the perfect spot for a romantic evening. Be it a first date, a celebration of an anniversary, New Year's Eve, or Valentine's Day. Each of our locations has cozy and secluded booths, and the four-course meal at The Melting Pot is served at a leisurely pace, allowing plenty of time for intimate conversation and cuddling. So come on down, and treat your special someone to a fondue experience that they will never forget!

The Original

8 ounces milk chocolate, finely chopped
2 tablespoons heavy cream
2 tablespoons chunky peanut butter

Serves 4 to 6

Combine the chocolate and cream in the top of a double boiler set over simmering water. Heat until the chocolate is melted, stirring constantly; or combine the chocolate and cream in a microwave-safe bowl and microwave until melted, stirring every 30 to 45 seconds. Be careful not to let the chocolate burn. Pour into a warm fondue pot. Add the peanut butter and stir gently until blended. Keep fondue warm over low heat.

Types of Chocolate—Milk

Milk chocolate is made of chocolate liquor mixed with milk and sugar. It has a creamier, smoother texture and a sweeter, milder flavor than dark chocolate. Milk chocolate melts fairly evenly and its milder taste makes it a great base for mixing with sweet liquors and other additives, such as peanut butter or marshmallow creme. Of course, milk chocolate is also just as delicious in its purest form—with nothing added!

Heavenly Chocolate Fondue

4 ounces dark chocolate,
   finely chopped
4 ounces caramel ice cream topping
2 tablespoons peanut butter
1/2 teaspoon 151 rum
2 tablespoons chopped chocolate
   sandwich cookies

Serves 4 to 6

Melt the chocolate in the top of a double boiler set over simmering water, stirring constantly; or place the chocolate in a microwave-safe bowl and microwave until melted, stirring every 30 to 45 seconds. Be careful not to let the chocolate burn. Pour into a warm fondue pot. Add the caramel and peanut butter and stir gently until blended. Add the rum to the pot and ignite carefully, using a long wooden match or lighter. Allow the flame to burn out and stir gently to combine. Sprinkle with the cookie crumbs. Keep fondue warm over low heat.

What Our Guests Say

"Being new to your restaurant, we were having problems deciding what to order. Our server made some great recommendations. We even purchased a fondue pot to give my sister as a Christmas gift! Rarely have either one of us ever been treated so well in a restaurant."

—Tim Thomas
Memphis, Tennessee

The Flaming Turtle

12 ounces milk chocolate,
　　finely chopped
2 tablespoons heavy cream
$1/4$ cup caramel ice cream topping
1 tablespoon 151 rum
3 tablespoons chopped pecans

Serves 4 to 6

Combine the chocolate and cream in the top of a double boiler set over simmering water. Heat until the chocolate is melted, stirring constantly; or combine the chocolate and cream in a microwave-safe bowl and microwave until melted, stirring every 30 to 45 seconds. Be careful not to let the chocolate burn. Pour into a warm fondue pot. Pour the caramel into the center of the chocolate mixture. Do not stir. Add the rum to the pot and ignite carefully, using a long wooden match or lighter. Allow the flame to burn out and stir gently to combine. Sprinkle with the pecans. Keep fondue warm over low heat.

Finding the Perfect Fondue Pot—Cheese and Chocolate

Ceramic or earthenware pots are usually preferred for making cheese or chocolate fondue at home, although delicious fondues of any type can also be made in a metal pot. Ceramic pots are available in a variety of colors, sizes, and even shapes—so it shouldn't be hard to find one you like. Ceramic pots should be heated with a low flame. Fondue sets generally come with a burning apparatus, but, in a pinch, a tea light or small candle will usually do the trick!

A Deep, Abiding Passion for Chocolate Fondue

Peanut Butter and Jelly Fondue

8 ounces dark chocolate,
  finely chopped
2 tablespoons heavy cream
2 tablespoons raspberry liqueur
2 teaspoons peanut butter

Serves 4 to 6

Combine the chocolate and cream in the top of a double boiler set over simmering water. Heat until the chocolate is melted, stirring constantly; or combine the chocolate and cream in a microwave-safe bowl and microwave until melted, stirring every 30 to 45 seconds. Be careful not to let the chocolate burn. Pour into a warm fondue pot. Add the liqueur and peanut butter and stir gently to combine. Keep fondue warm over low heat.

Children's Fondue Party Tips

Adults aren't the only ones who love to fondue—so let your kids get in on the action! For children's fondue parties it's usually best to stick to cheese and chocolate. When it's time for dessert, present kids with their own bowls of chocolate fondue and different mix-ins, such as cookies, marshmallows, and candy. That way, each child can customize his chocolate fondue and use his fingers for dipping instead of sharp forks, provided you make sure the chocolate is cool enough first!

Snickers Bar Fondue

8 ounces milk chocolate,
  finely chopped
1/2 cup caramel ice cream topping
2 teaspoons chunky peanut butter

Serves 4 to 6

Melt the chocolate in the top of a double boiler set over simmering water, stirring constantly; or place the chocolate in a microwave-safe bowl and microwave until melted, stirring every 30 to 45 seconds. Be careful not to let the chocolate burn. Pour into a warm fondue pot. Add the caramel and peanut butter and stir gently until blended. Keep fondue warm over low heat.

New Year's Eve

New Year's Eve can be either a boisterous or romantic holiday, depending on whether or not you are with a group or want to spend some quality alone time with a special someone. No matter who you want to ring in the New Year with, The Melting Pot can accommodate. After all, what better way to count down to midnight than with a glass of Champagne and a pot of warm chocolate fondue?

A Deep, Abiding Passion for Chocolate Fondue

Strawberries and Cream Fondue

1/2 cup quartered fresh strawberries
Confectioners' sugar to taste
4 1/2 ounces (3/4 cup) finely chopped
    white chocolate
1/4 cup heavy cream
1/4 cup raspberry liqueur

Serves 4 to 6

Place the strawberries in a food processor or blender and process until smooth. Pour into a small bowl. Add the confectioners' sugar and mix well. Combine the chocolate and cream in a fondue pot set over low heat. Heat until the chocolate is melted, stirring constantly. Add the liqueur and stir gently to combine. Swirl the strawberry purée gently on the surface of the fondue. Keep fondue warm over low heat.

Types of Chocolate—White
White chocolate is made up of sugar, cocoa butter, and milk solids. Unlike dark or milk chocolate, white chocolate contains neither chocolate liquor nor cocoa solids. White chocolate often contains vanilla. White chocolate has the same consistency as milk chocolate, but a less intense flavor, which allows white chocolate fondue to take on more of the flavors of liquors, nuts, or any other mix-ins.

Coconut Rum Fondue

8 ounces milk chocolate,
    finely chopped
1/2 cup mascarpone cheese
2 tablespoons coconut rum

Serves 4 to 6

Melt the chocolate in the top of a double boiler set over simmering water, stirring constantly; or place the chocolate in a microwave-safe bowl and microwave until melted, stirring every 30 to 45 seconds. Be careful not to let the chocolate burn. Pour into a warm fondue pot. Add the cheese and stir gently until blended. Add the rum and stir gently to combine. Keep fondue warm over low heat.

Tiramisu Fondue

1 cup mascarpone cheese
2 tablespoons rum
4 ounces dark chocolate,
    finely chopped
3 tablespoons espresso, or
    1 tablespoon instant
    coffee granules
1 tablespoon superfine sugar
    (optional)

Serves 4 to 6

Combine the cheese and rum in a fondue pot set over low heat. Heat until the cheese is melted and the mixture is blended, stirring constantly. Add the chocolate and heat until blended, stirring constantly. Stir in the espresso and sugar. If substituting coffee granules for the espresso, dissolve the granules in 3 tablespoons hot water before adding to the fondue pot. Keep fondue warm over low heat.

Toffee Fondue

3 teaspoons cornstarch
2 tablespoons water
3 tablespoons light brown sugar
2 tablespoons butter, chopped
2 tablespoons corn syrup
3/4 cup evaporated milk
3 teaspoons chopped
    unsalted peanuts

Serves 4 to 6

Dissolve the cornstarch in the water in a small bowl. Combine the brown sugar, butter and corn syrup in a saucepan. Bring to a boil and boil for 1 minute, stirring constantly. Stir in the evaporated milk gently and return to a boil. Add the cornstarch mixture and cook until thickened, stirring constantly. Stir in the peanuts. Pour into a warm fondue pot. Keep fondue warm over low heat.

The Melting Pot in the News

"Brian Skedd was vacationing in Arizona when he first dined at The Melting Pot. He was impressed enough to make immediate plans to open the chain's second Massachusetts restaurant. Skedd, a longtime Westford resident, said he was taken with The Melting Pot before even tasting some of its dozen-plus different flavors of cheese and chocolate fondues. 'Before we even ate, we just walked in and were so impressed with the elegance of the atmosphere,' Skedd said."

—*The Sun*
Lowell, Massachusetts
January 17, 2007

White Chocolate Butterscotch Fondue

1 1/2 cups packed light brown sugar
3/4 cup light corn syrup
1/3 cup water
1/4 cup (1/2 stick) unsalted
   butter, chopped
1/3 cup heavy cream
1 teaspoon vanilla extract
4 ounces white chocolate,
   finely chopped

Serves 4 to 6

Combine the brown sugar, corn syrup and water in a small saucepan. Bring to a full boil, stirring occasionally. Reduce the heat to medium. Cook for 20 to 25 minutes, stirring occasionally. Remove from the heat. Add the butter and stir until melted. Add the cream and vanilla and stir until the mixture is blended. Add the white chocolate and stir until smooth. Pour into a warm fondue pot. Keep fondue warm over low heat.

Fondue Cooking Tips

The easiest way to cook fondue at home is to start it on the stove using a double boiler and then serve it in the fondue pot. Once your fondue has been transferred to the pot, never let it boil. Keep cheese and dessert fondues at a low temperature—about 120 degrees—using a tea light. When heating oil or broth for entrée fondues, keep the pot at about 375 degrees. To test the temperature, dip in a cube of bread. It should brown evenly in about 30 seconds.

A Deep, Abiding Passion for Chocolate Fondue

White Chocolate Apple Pie Fondue

8 ounces white chocolate,
    finely chopped
1/2 cup apple pie filling
2 tablespoons 151 rum
3 tablespoons graham cracker
    crumbs

Serves 4 to 6

Melt the chocolate in the top of a double boiler set over simmering water, stirring constantly; or place the chocolate in a microwave-safe bowl and microwave until melted, stirring every 30 to 45 seconds. Be careful not to let the chocolate burn. Pour into a warm fondue pot. Add the pie filling and stir gently to combine. Add the rum to the pot and ignite carefully, using a long wooden match or lighter. Allow the flame to burn out and stir gently to combine. Sprinkle with the graham cracker crumbs. Keep fondue warm over low heat.

 ### The Melting Pot in the News

"The Melting Pot is the ultimate experience for kids who love to dip their food, serving more than a dozen kinds of cheese, entrée, and dessert fondues. 'The concept of dipping prompts kids to try foods they may never have given a shot at home,' says Kendra Sartor, Vice President of Brand Development."

—*Child* magazine, April 2004

White Chocolate Praline Fondue

8 ounces white chocolate,
   finely chopped
1 tablespoon heavy cream
1/2 cup caramel ice cream
   topping, warmed
2 tablespoons bourbon
2 tablespoons 151 rum

Serves 4 to 6

Combine the chocolate and cream in the top of a double boiler set over simmering water. Heat until the chocolate is melted, stirring constantly; or combine the chocolate and cream in a microwave-safe bowl and microwave until melted, stirring every 30 to 45 seconds. Be careful not to let the chocolate burn. Pour into a warm fondue pot. Add the caramel and bourbon and gently swirl seven to ten times. Add the rum to the pot and ignite carefully, using a long wooden match or lighter. Allow the flame to burn out and stir gently to combine. Keep fondue warm over low heat.

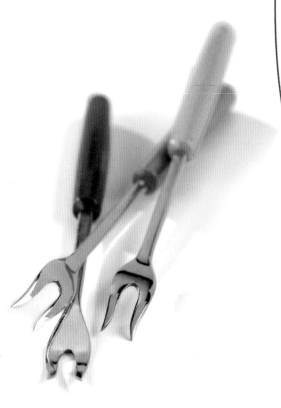

The Melting Pot and St. Jude— The Perfect Pair

The Melting Pot is proud to support the St. Jude Children's Research Hospital in the fight against childhood cancer. The Melting Pot sponsors fundraising programs at all of its locations, as well as donating funds directly to St. Jude. The Melting Pot has also developed the *Fondue a Cure for Childhood Cancer* promotion. With every purchase of The Melting Pot's fondue chocolate bar, $1 will be given to the hospital. The bars are available at all of the Melting Pot restaurants and online.

Cocktails and Coffees

A cocktail with appetizers, a bottle of wine with the entrée, a mug of coffee with dessert — the ideal beverage pairing elevates fondue from a good meal to a memorable experience.

The Melting Pot has always emphasized beverages that can hold their own. Our bartenders have created signature cocktails like the Chocolate Fontini and the Zen Tini. An extensive menu of modern takes on classic after-dinner drinks — including rich coffees, flavored cappuccinos, espressos, and creamy Irish coffees — has something that everyone can enjoy. These delicious drinks are easy to re-create at home so you can enjoy them whenever you fondue.

Because of the special relationship between wine and cheese, a great bottle of wine is always a wonderful beverage choice. The Melting Pot has nurtured that special relationship by developing an extensive wine list. In fact, fifty-three of The Melting Pot's franchises have won *Wine Spectator* awards to date. Whenever serving fondue, it never hurts to have an extra bottle on hand!

Love Martini

1 strawberry
1 1/2 ounces coconut-flavored rum
1 ounce peach schnapps
2 ounces cranberry juice

Serves 1

Remove the stem from the strawberry. Slice the strawberry and cut a small "v" in the top of each slice to create a heart shape. Place several ice cubes in a cocktail shaker and add the rum, schnapps and cranberry juice. Shake until chilled. Strain into a chilled martini glass and garnish with the strawberry slices.

Valentine's Day

With The Melting Pot's reputation for romance, it is no surprise that it has become a popular Valentine's Day destination. Most locations even offer an exclusive Valentine's Day menu with special cheeses and chocolates, as well as optional floral or balloon arrangements, gift bags, and professional photographs that you can arrange to have waiting for your beloved on the table when you arrive. But Valentine's Day reservations fill up fast—so make sure to call well in advance!

Purple Haze

¹/₂ ounce gin
¹/₂ ounce vodka
¹/₂ ounce rum
2 ounces sweet and sour mix
1 ounce lemon-lime soda
¹/₂ ounce black raspberry liqueur
1 lemon slice

Serves 1

Pour the gin, vodka, rum, sweet and sour mix, soda and liqueur in a glass over ice. Stir to combine. Squeeze the lemon into the drink.

Cosmo Blanco

1¹/₄ ounces citrus-flavored vodka
³/₄ ounce Cointreau
2 ounces white cranberry juice
Lemon twist

Serves 1

Place several ice cubes in a cocktail shaker and add the vodka, Cointreau and cranberry juice. Shake until chilled. Strain into a chilled martini glass. Place a lemon twist on the rim to garnish.

Zen Tini

1 part green tea liqueur
2 parts vodka
1 splash of lime juice

Serves 1

Place several ice cubes in a cocktail shaker and add the liqueur and vodka. Shake until chilled. Strain into a martini glass. Pour a splash of lime juice into the glass.

Island Chai Martini

2 ounces chai cream liqueur
1 ounce crème de cacao
1 ounce coconut-flavored rum
1 ounce pineapple juice

Serves 1

Place several ice cubes in a cocktail shaker and add the liqueur, crème de cacao, rum and pineapple juice. Shake until chilled. Strain into a martini glass.

137

Erv's Asian Pear Martini

1 ounce Asian pear sake
1/2 ounce citrus-flavored vodka
1/2 ounce peach schnapps
1/2 ounce sour apple schnapps
1 thin slice Asian pear

Serves 1

Place several ice cubes in a cocktail shaker and add the sake, vodka and schnapps. Shake until chilled. Strain into a glass and garnish with the pear slice.

Fun Fondue Fork-lore— The Forfeit

Since fondue became a popular party food, many fun customs have sprung up around the pot, such as "the forfeit." When a group is dipping bread into cheese fondue and a woman drops her bread into the pot, she has to kiss the man sitting to her left. If a man drops his bread, he has to buy or prepare the next round of drinks. And if any person drops a cube of bread in twice, he or she has to host the next fondue party!

138

Strawberry Basil Lemonade

3 strawberries, stems removed
5 basil leaves
1 1/2 ounces strawberry-flavored
   vodka
2 tablespoons strawberry purée
14 ounces lemonade
Whole strawberry (optional)
Basil leaf (optional)

Serves 1

Combine the strawberries, basil, vodka and strawberry purée in a cocktail shaker and mash with a wooden spoon. Add several ice cubes and shake for 15 seconds. Pour into a glass. Fill with the lemonade and stir to combine. Garnish with a strawberry and/or a basil leaf.

What Our Guests Say

"My husband and I celebrated the anniversary of our first date at The Melting Pot. The restaurant, from the design to the intimacy to the wine selection, was outstanding. We were visited by the manager on duty. I wanted a wine that you do not serve, but he suggested a substitute, which was great. Beyond the wine, we were impressed with his sincerity and dedication to elevating our experience—he even made our cheese fondue for us!"

—Darrell and Taryn Walker
Lyndhurst, Ohio

Watermelon Margarita

$^1/_2$ cup sugar

$^1/_2$ cup water

1 teaspoon grated lime zest

Coarse salt to taste

1 lime wedge

1 cup watermelon purée
  (see Note below)

2 tablespoons fresh lime juice

4 ounces premium 100 percent
  agave tequila

1 ounce orange-flavored liqueur
  (Grand Marnier or Triple Sec
  recommended)

1 cup ice

  Serves 1

Chill a margarita glass in the freezer for 30 minutes. Combine the sugar, water and lime zest in a small saucepan. Bring to a boil over medium heat, stirring constantly until the sugar is dissolved. Remove from the heat and let stand until cooled to room temperature. Strain into a container and discard the lime zest. You may prepare the syrup to this point and chill, covered, until ready to use.

Spread salt on a small flat plate. Moisten the rim of the margarita glass with the lime wedge. Invert the glass onto the plate and rotate gently to cover the rim evenly with the salt, shaking off the excess.

Combine 2 tablespoons of the lime syrup, the watermelon purée, lime juice, tequila, liqueur and ice in a cocktail shaker. Shake for 1 minute or until frothy and well-chilled. Strain into the prepared glass and garnish with the lime wedge. Store any unused lime syrup in the refrigerator for up to 1 week.

Note—To prepare watermelon purée, remove and discard the seeds from a watermelon. Cut the watermelon into chunks. Place in a blender and process until puréed. Store any unused watermelon purée in the refrigerator for up to 2 days.

Black and Blue Mojito

2 tablespoons blackberries
2 tablespoons blueberries
2 or 3 mint leaves
1 teaspoon raw sugar
1 tablespoon fresh lime juice
3 to 4 ounces white rum
Crushed ice
Soda water
1 lime slice

Serves 1

Combine the blackberries, blueberries, mint, sugar and lime juice in a cocktail shaker and mash with a mortar or the back of a wooden spoon. Add the rum and crushed ice and shake until chilled. Pour into a tall glass. Pour a splash of soda water into the glass and garnish with the lime slice.

Cooking with Alcohol

Wine and beer have always been a part of the fondue tradition, and the use of different wines and beers helps give each pot of fondue its own unique flavor. Always select a wine or beer for your fondue that you would drink as well, since the flavor will be infused into the cheese. Beer is best paired with Cheddar or Gouda cheeses, while white wine or Champagne is delicious in Swiss cheese fondue. A good red wine makes an excellent base for an entrée fondue when combined with broth. Dessert liquors are especially delicious when mixed into a pot of chocolate fondue at the end of a meal. Don't worry about the kids when it comes to cooking with alcohol—it burns off and is completely safe for them.

Paradise Punch (AKA Joanie's Tipsy Turtle)

1/4 ounce 151 rum
1/4 ounce light rum
1/4 ounce dark rum
1/4 ounce coconut-flavored rum
1/4 ounce spiced rum
1/4 ounce crème de banana
4 ounces orange juice
1/2 ounce pineapple juice
Grenadine
1 pineapple wedge

Serves 1

Combine the rums, banana liqueur, orange juice, pineapple juice and a splash of grenadine in a tall glass filled with ice and stir gently. Garnish with the pineapple wedge.

Sangria

20 ounces red wine
5 ounces Triple Sec
2 1/2 ounces brandy
5 ounces pineapple juice
5 teaspoons sugar
5 dashes of cinnamon
5 ounces (or more) lemon-lime soda

Serves 6 to 8

Combine the wine, Triple Sec, brandy, pineapple juice, sugar and cinnamon in a pitcher and mix well. Add enough soda to fill the pitcher. Pour into glasses filled with ice.

Sangria Blanco

4 ounces water

1/4 cup sugar

3 cinnamon sticks

8 ounces unsweetened apple juice

8 ounces fresh orange juice

1 (750-milliliter) bottle white wine
  (chardonnay recommended)

1 small apple, thinly sliced

1 orange, thinly sliced

1 banana, sliced

Sparkling water

Serves 6 to 8

Combine the water, sugar and cinnamon sticks in a small saucepan. Simmer for 5 minutes, stirring occasionally. Remove and discard the cinnamon sticks. Let mixture stand until cool. Combine with the apple juice, orange juice and wine in a pitcher and chill for 4 hours or longer. Serve over ice in glasses. Garnish each glass with some of the fruit slices. Pour a splash of sparkling water into each glass.

What Our Guests Say

"My friends and I went to The Melting Pot to celebrate a birthday. Brandon was the manager and was wonderful. I arrived early and sat in the lobby talking with him. I knew he had other things to do, so the fact he helped pass the time until my friends came was extremely nice. He also showed us to our table. When he realized it was my friend's birthday, he made her a raspberry martini. He even floated a candle in it so she could make a wish. At the end, we decided against dessert because we were so full. But Brandon wouldn't take no for an answer and decided to bring us some chocolate—on him. I have never been taken care of like I was in Gaithersburg."

—Kym Danowski
Gaithersburg, Maryland

147

Chocolate Fontini

¹/₂ ounce chocolate syrup
1 ounce chocolate liqueur
¹/₂ ounce Kahlúa
¹/₂ ounce Irish cream liqueur
¹/₂ ounce blackberry syrup
Splash of heavy cream or
    half-and-half

Serves 1

Chill a martini glass. Drizzle the chocolate syrup inside the glass. Combine the chocolate liqueur, Kahlúa, Irish cream liqueur, blackberry syrup and cream in a small pitcher and mix well. Pour into the prepared glass.

Beverages

The Melting Pot has specialty cocktails that perfectly complement each course of the fondue experience, as well as an extensive wine list. In fact, fifty-three of The Melting Pot's 132 franchises have won *Wine Spectator* awards. We are constantly on the lookout for new vintages and new ways of serving wines, such as wine flights that allow guests to sample a different wine with each course. In addition, almost all locations have a fully stocked bar that can cater to any taste.

Cocktails and Coffees

White Chocolate Cappuccino

6 ounces cappuccino
1¼ ounces white chocolate liqueur

Serves 1

Pour the cappuccino into a mug. Stir in the liqueur. Serve warm.

Espressotini

2 ounces cold espresso
2 ounces vodka
½ ounce coffee-flavored liqueur
½ ounce raspberry liqueur
¼ ounce simple syrup
3 coffee beans (optional)

Serves 1

Place several ice cubes in a cocktail shaker and add the espresso, vodka, liqueurs and simple syrup. Shake until chilled. Strain into a martini glass. Garnish with the coffee beans.

Café Reggae

6 ounces freshly brewed coffee
1/2 ounce dark rum
1/2 ounce Tia Maria
1/2 ounce dark crème de cacao
Whipped cream

Serves 1

Pour the coffee into a mug. Add the rum and liqueurs and mix well. Top with a dollop of whipped cream. Serve warm.

Siberian Warm-Up

6 ounces freshly brewed coffee
1 teaspoon sugar
3/4 ounce brandy
3/4 ounce Kahlúa
Whipped cream

Serves 1

Pour the coffee into a mug. Add the sugar, brandy and Kahlúa and mix well. Top with a dollop of whipped cream. Serve warm.

Hot-Hot-Hot Toddy

16 ounces orange juice
8 ounces cranberry juice
1/4 cup sugar
1 teaspoon whole cloves
1 (3-inch) cinnamon stick
1 teaspoon grated orange zest
Orange slices
Whole cloves

Serves 6

Combine the orange juice, cranberry juice, sugar, 1 teaspoon cloves, the cinnamon stick and orange zest in a saucepan over low heat. Bring to a boil and simmer for 5 minutes, stirring occasionally. Strain into a heated bowl or pitcher. Pour into heavy glasses or mugs. Top each drink with an orange slice studded with additional cloves. Serve warm.

Mulled Wine

1 (750-milliliter) bottle dry
   red wine
Dash of cinnamon
Dash of cloves
Dash of nutmeg
Sugar to taste

Serves 4 to 6

Combine the wine, cinnamon, cloves, nutmeg and sugar in a saucepan. Heat until warm. Pour into heavy glasses or mugs.

152

Index

Dip into Something Different®

**A collection of recipes
from our fondue pot to yours**

For additional copies of our cookbook, please
visit your local Melting Pot restaurant, or you may
visit us online at www.meltingpot.com.